"If *Unleashing the Power of Encouragement* does not encourage you, I don't know what will! Reid does a wonderful job of intersecting an authentic perspective with the truth of God's Word, challenging us to know and understand the difference between a life of success verses a life of significance. He helps us see it's not what you get out of life that matters most; it's what you give! As one who has been given the gift of encouragement, I have been encouraged! *Unleashing the Power of Encouragement* is a must read if you truly desire to live a full life and make a difference in this world!

Dave Dravecky
Former Major League baseball player, Author
President and founder of Endurance with Jan and Dave Dravecky


Reid Lamport was an inspiration to me twenty-six years ago as a high school football player, and even more today as the forty-four-year-old president of two hospitals in Northeast Ohio. He encouraged me to work harder than anyone else; he encouraged me to work smarter than anyone else; but, most importantly, he encouraged me to celebrate wins in life along the way. After reading *Unleashing the Power of Encouragement*, you will desire to encourage your family members, friends and co-workers to pursue their passions and be the best they can be every day.

Robert G. David
President, University Hospitals, Conneaut and Geneva Medical Centers


Reid Lamport's unique, God-given skills as a coach, mentor and Christian spiritual guide have been empirically verified throughout the thirty years that he and I have shared our common faith in Christ. This superb literary work on the art and theology of encouragement chronicles the divinely inspired tools that Reid has successfully used in the momentous instruction and moral support of numerous young men and women in meeting the significant challenges they will face in the various arenas of both sports and life. One might say that Reid is a modern-day Barnabas – "son of encouragement."

Charles H. McGowen, MD
Author of *In Six Days; Let's Talk About Heaven;* and *Dissecting the Truth.*

# Unleashing the Power
## of Encouragement

Reid Lamport

Pat—

Thanks for encouraging and inspiring my daughter, it's helped her become the woman she is today.

Rud

To God Be The Glory

# Acknowledgments

*Your love has given me great joy and encouragement.*
*(Philemon 1:7)*

Where do I begin? It probably wouldn't be a bad idea to start with the Holy Spirit since this entire endeavor was His inspiration. To God Almighty, I say, "Thank You." Thank You for how patient You are with me. Thank You for Your unconditional love despite my conditional faith. For Your strength and Your encouragement to persevere in writing this book when my personal resources ran dry; for Your wisdom when I could no longer think; and for Your energy when I could no longer type, thank You. But most of all, Father, thank You for Your grace, the one thing that defines and exemplifies "encouragement" far better than any book ever could.

Thank You, Father, for leading me to Mary Busha, my nominee for "Editor of the Year." Her ability to take the words of this old coach and preacher and turn them into something others might find inspiring is nothing short of remarkable. She has been a great motivator, friend and sister in the Lord.

For my children who have been great encouragers throughout this three-year process, I say, thank You. They took a sincere interest in this book, and their personal involvement has meant more to me than they could ever know. To them I say, "I am so proud to be your father."

Thank You, dear God, for the fifty-nine years I have had the privilege of being the son of Beatrice Lamport. One would be hard-pressed to find a more loving, compassionate and unselfish person this side of heaven. Without her prayers, I shudder to think just where her son would have ended up.

Finally, Lord, thank You for Michele. It's an amazing thing when you're married to your best friend. Her beauty, both inward and outward, attracts me more today than yesterday. "Honey, your patience with me and your belief in me for this project could never be measured. I am so looking forward to spending the rest of our days here together!"

# Contents

# Introduction

*Unleashing the Power of Encouragement* is written to bring to light the enormous potential each of us hold in becoming people who can effect change in the hearts and lives of all those we know. The ability we possess for enhancing peoples' lives and increasing their self-esteem has been under lock and key long enough; it's time we begin taking a proactive role in doing something about it.

Personally I'm tired of seeing my friends, family, and those I work and worship with wallowing around in mediocrity when I know raising their sense of worth and their quality of life can be but one or two words away. The sad part is, while everyone carries with them this capacity to effectively change lives, so few ever carry it out to fruition. I can also tell you that while the risks in carrying this out are virtually nonexistent, the rewards can be incalculable. In these times of economic crisis, where are you going to get that kind of return on investment?

The best part is, when we seek to encourage others, we fulfill a purpose for our lives, a very specific and significant purpose. Contrary to what the world constantly tells us, our purpose for living is not seeing how much temporary pleasure we can squeeze out of life. Our call and our purpose are finding ways of enhancing the lives of those around us. I have discovered that nothing is as cost effective for enhancing the lives of people like our encouragement. While it may sound as though I'm overstating the power of the words we say to each other, I can tell you that at least one other person agrees with me. Maybe you've heard of him. King Solomon?

*The tongue has the power of life and death.*
*(Proverbs 18:21)*

I'm not sure how you can overstate life and death. By living to encourage others, we ultimately discover something for ourselves along the way; something much greater than self-attained happiness. Self-attained happiness brings with it nothing that's lasting nor fulfilling. Fulfillment, true fulfillment comes only when we're seeking something a little more significant.

> *But seek first his kingdom and his righteousness,*
> *and all these things will be given to you as well.*
> *(Matthew 6:33)*

When we follow God's principles for life, it's amazing how blessed we become in the process. By taking the spotlight off ourselves and making it about someone else, God has a way of making sure our needs are tended to. It's really about faith. Do we trust Him enough to take care of us or don't we? Those who are constantly looking to validate themselves through things and accomplishments don't trust enough in the validation of our heavenly Father.

While there is nothing wrong with setting out to accomplish certain goals, there is something wrong in the motivation of many who do. If the purpose in attaining goals is to impress others or to elevate yourself above others, you're more than likely headed for some major disappointment. Attempting to please and impress others will wear you out faster than anything else you can ever do. It's because there will never be an end to the process. Just when you think you have completed your mission, here comes someone else you have failed to impress. However, if your goal is to elevate the confidence and the self-esteem of others, every word of encouragement you speak will translate to victory.

"You're an amazing person, you know that?" *Bam! You just hit a homerun.*

"I've never been more proud of someone in my life!" *Bull's eye!*

"I can't tell you what your friendship means to me!" *He's at the ten, the five, touchdown!*

The remarkable thing about validating other people is the satisfaction *you* receive when you're lifting them up.

*For everyone who exalts himself will be humbled,*
*and he who humbles himself will be exalted.*
*(Luke 14:11)*

I can honestly say, since I have been actively and consciously *unleashing the power of encouragement*, I've never felt more exalted. It's a powerful tool, encouragement. It has the capability of improving the lives of everyone you meet! Give it a try, thirty days, no charge. If you're not completely satisfied after this trial period, you can simply take back all your encouragement and return to whatever it was you were doing that gave your life more purpose and satisfaction. I'm betting the only thing you'll be doing thirty days from now, however, is seeking new ways of unleashing this newly discovered power.

# Author's Note

I think it's important for you to understand the background for this book. In all honesty, I wasn't looking to write a book on encouragement. Actually, I wasn't looking to write a book on anything. Trust me; my life is much too busy. I was merely swimming laps in the pool at the YMCA one day, preparing for my upcoming hip-replacement surgery, when I experienced the overwhelming sensation that I was to author a book.

My workouts in the pool usually include some time in prayer and meditation, and this particular session began much like all the others. I have an underwater *iPod* loaded with praise and worship music that helps considerably in getting my focus off me and onto God. We have had some great conversations in the water, the Lord and I. I guess it's OK to call them conversations even though it's me doing ninety-nine percent of the talking. Not this time, however; this time I was on the receiving end. God spoke so profoundly into my spirit that for an instant I thought what I was hearing was coming from the *iPod*. I can't explain it any other way than that. While it may not have been audible, it was nonetheless personal and it was profound.

The word I received was to write a book, but not just any book. It was to be a very specific book, a book dealing with the subject of encouragement. My first reaction was to think, *is this me or is this God?* The mere notion of writing a book at that time was overwhelming to say the least. I attempted one of the more common practices I resort to when presented with a *God-thing* that seems beyond my capabilities; I attempted to change the subject. A futile attempt I may add. It was an impression that just wouldn't let go. I also remember explicitly that I was to begin writing this book when I returned home from the hospital following my surgery, putting to productive use my six weeks of rehabilitation.

One thing I remember wondering as I finished my shower and got dressed, and began the drive home; I wondered why I wasn't feeling nervous or anxious. Normally I would have already begun to doubt my ability to do something this grand, but such was not the case. Instead I began to think with excitement the possibilities involved in writing a book. One such possibility was that large numbers of people would have the opportunity to read what God desires me to write. I pulled in the garage, parked my car, walked in the house, dropped my gym bag on the floor and announced to my wife, Michele, "Honey, we need to buy a laptop!"

I'm not sure how most wives would respond to their husband telling them it was God's desire for him to write a book, but after two minutes of explaining to Michele my encounter in the pool, her response was, "I think *Best Buy* has some really good deals on computers right now. If you want, we can run over after dinner." How can you not love a woman like that? Sensing an opportunity I may never get again had presented itself, I quickly added that it was possible I might have also heard God say something about a new set of golf clubs to help in rehabbing the hip. After I've had time to think back on it, I should have started with the clubs and moved to the laptop.

Well, there you have it; the story behind *Unleashing the Power of Encouragement*. I'm happy to announce that throughout the process of writing, editing, and having this book published, I have never once felt anxiety over this endeavor. Why should I? If someone tells me they didn't find it enjoyable, I'll just tell them to take it up with God; it was *His* idea.

The truth is, I pray you find it to be inspiring, because I believe it to be the truly inspired who seek to enact change in the hearts and lives of people. And nothing else can enact change like encouragement. My hope is for every one hundred of you who read this book, one thousand others become encouraged.

**Part 1**

# Encouragement Made Simple

*Understanding the purpose behind encouragement and how it can be applied can go a long way in motivating us to make it a priority in life.*

# 1

# What Is Encouragement?

*Take courage! It is I. Don't be afraid.*
*(Matthew 14:27)*

**En-courage** \in-'ker-ij *ME encoragen, fr. MF encoragier, fr. OF, fr. en +courage. To make, (or to)* **put in courage***. To inspire, spur on another.*

S imply put, encouragement is the act of supplying courage to someone else by way of doing or saying something to inspire them. While it may sound rather trivial to say we can give courage to someone else simply by inspiring them verbally, it would be a mistake to downplay its importance.

Is there really a need for people to have their courage increased? Are you kidding me? Look around you. Fear is at an all-time high; people seem to be afraid of everything. It's gotten to the point where we now have names for all our fears. There are literally hundreds of fears officially listed as phobias.

*Papyrophobia* is the fear of paper. There are people who actually fear paper! Wood bark soaked, softened and rolled into thin sheets of printing material; now there's something that will send shock waves up your spine. There's *bibliophobia*, the fear of books. Two groups of people right here who unfortunately won't be getting any of this information until it comes out as an audio book.

Now we're not going to get rid of everyone's fears; nor should we try. Some fears are healthy like *selachophobia*, the fear of sharks. This fear keeps us from diving into ocean water at the first sign of a dorsal fin. This next one I'm going to take some heat for from my good friend Dr. Jeffrey Logan. It's *dentophobia,* the fear of, that's right, dentists. A little fear of dentists can motivate us to brush regularly and watch what we eat, right? That's not all bad. Here's one some members of my congregation seem to be battling from time to time: *homilophobia*, the fear of sermons.

While we poke fun at some of the more outlandish fears people appear to suffer from, some fears, although many times irrational to us, are very real and can keep the children of God from appreciating and enjoying life. The truth is, everyone fears something whether it's rational or not, and while certain fears may seem silly to us, those suffering from fear know how devastating it can be.

God has given each of His children something to overcome any and all fear. He has given us courage.

> *But Christ is faithful as a son over God's house.*
> *And we are his house, if we hold on to our courage*
> *and the hope of which we boast.*
> *(Hebrews 3:6)*

The author of Hebrews instructs us to "hold on" to our courage. In order to hold on to something, we must first be in possession of it. The reality is, every child of God possesses a measure of courage sufficient to conquer the fear we face in our lives. That courage is manifested through the Holy Spirit. Sometimes certain events take place in our lives that cause us to question or second-guess our courage. That's when we need one another to remind us that what God has given us is more than enough. The most effective way to remind each other is through encouragement.

**Trust in the courage you already have**

Let's take a look at one of the most fear-filled characters of all time: the Cowardly Lion from the *Wizard of Oz*. The one thing he wanted more than anything else was what? Courage. He felt by obtaining courage it would complete him as a lion. After all, lions are supposed to be the epitome of courage. It's pretty tough being King of the Forest without it. Courage for the Cowardly Lion should have been second nature, an intrinsic characteristic that merely surfaced without effort. This lion, however, seemed to be afraid of everything.

Now we all know how the story plays out. The lion discovers he wasn't void of courage at all; he had plenty of it. He merely needed *en-couraged* by the "All Powerful Wizard." The lion was looking for something physical, something tangible to transform him into this raging beast. Little did he know, all that was needed was a little validation from the Wizard, a bogus wizard at that. He merely needed to remind the lion of all the times he had already demonstrated courage. The Wizard pointed out instances in the lion's life where it took great courage on his part to complete the task at hand. He convinced the lion, through his encouragement, that he didn't need more courage at all; he just needed to trust in the courage he already possessed.

The conversion from Cowardly Lion to the Courageous Lion came after the Wizard hung the "Medal of Courage" on his chest; although it would have been more accurate to call it the "Medal of Encouragement." We know there wasn't anything magical in that medal; it simply served as a reminder. The Wizard, being a mortal man himself, wasn't the source of courage either; he merely served as the encourager and was able to bring forth the lion's courage by just reminding him he had been in possession of it all along. That dose of affirmation alone inspired him and restored not only his self-esteem, but his confidence as well. As the Wizard hung that medal on his chest, he spoke courage into the Lion:

> *For meritorious conduct, extraordinary valor, conspicuous*
> *bravery against wicked witches I award you the triple cross. You*
> *are now a member of the Legion of Courage.*

You remember the rest of the story. The lion's attitude and demeanor were transformed from that point on simply by being validated through encouragement. Now I know it was just a movie, but the principle of encouragement holds just as true for all of us on this side of Hollywood. I know how often I have to be reminded of the courage I possess. It's not as though I live in fear, however, I admit there are times when my confidence gets shaken and I begin to question my own abilities by listening to the enemy. When that happens, my courage can return, just like the lion's, with a single word of encouragement. The source of that courage, though, is what separates us from the lion. While his Wizard couldn't actually supply him with courage, we have One who can.

> *But Jesus said immediately to them:*
> *"Take courage! It is I. Don't be afraid."*
> *(Matthew 14:27)*

Jesus was commanding His disciples to take hold of the courage He desired to give them. What is important for us to understand as people susceptible to becoming fearful is that we have the availability, just as the disciples did, of entering into the presence of the Lord as often as necessary and taking our place among God's Legion of Courage. And once there, unlike alcohol, unlike drugs, unlike magic potions, unlike the Wizard in the movie,

> *My God will meet all your needs according*
> *to his glorious riches in Christ Jesus.*
> *(Philippians 4:19)*

That's the best part; we don't have to try out or test anything else other than God. There's no one else, or any place else, that can meet our needs. Besides, God's record for meeting the needs of His children is impeccable. Now if we take a look at the Scarecrow and the Tin Man, we see both of them, just like their friend the Lion, were looking for something they already possessed. They, too, allowed the enemy's voice to convince them they were lacking what they needed to be made whole. The Wizard however restored them as well by reminding them, through his encouraging words, they were already in possession of both brains and a heart. It took but a few moments of sincere encouragement to reinstate the self-confidence the Lion's friends thought was missing.

**Help is but a prayer away**
As children of God, what we have to understand is this: We have been created whole. We are not lacking anything in order to become complete. Not one of us is in need of a trip to the Wizard. Surely there are times our confidence is going to get shaken. We may experience what seems like one defeat after another, however we cannot allow the voice of the enemy to convince us that while everyone else has it all together, we're out there floundering alone and helpless. Our help in these times is but a prayer away. And don't be surprised if that prayer is answered by someone God has sent to encourage us.

God uses those who have made themselves available, and while I'll never say God can't speak audibly to His children, I will say it seems as though He more frequently uses other children to speak for Him. Don't dismiss the idea that your most recent encouragement, even though it came from a friend, didn't originate from God. It's quite possible the words spoken to validate and encourage you were coined right in His very throne room. After all, who knows better what we need and when we need it than the One who created us? All too often, however, we're looking for God to show up like the Wizard on the big screen and speak to us through the smoke, the flashes of lightning, and the sound of trumpets with the declaration, "Thus saith the Lord!" More often than not He comes to us in less conspicuous ways.

Remember the prophet Elijah, in 1 Kings 19, fleeing Mount Horeb, feeling alone and afraid? There was nothing Elijah needed at that time more than courage. The voice of an angel told him to get up and go stand on the mountain and wait on the Lord. Elijah obeyed and waited as a "great and powerful wind" tore the mountains apart and shattered the rocks; Elijah waited as an "earthquake" shook the foundations of the earth; and Elijah waited still as "fire" appeared before him. But he quickly discovered the Lord was not in any of those.

> *The Lord was not in the wind. After the wind there was an earth-*
> *quake, but the Lord was not in the earthquake. After the earth-*
> *quake came a fire but the Lord was not in the fire. After the fire*
> *came a gentle whisper.*
> *(1 Kings 19:11-12)*

We learn, of course, it was in the gentle whisper that the Lord appeared. His word to Elijah restored the prophet's courage and enabled him to fulfill God's plan for his life. In reality, we have potential whisperers around us every day. People who need only remind us, by way of encouragement, what God wants us to hear, things such as:

"You can do it."

"You are capable."

"You do possess the necessary courage, the right amount of brains, or the warmest of hearts."

What a great lesson, especially for those of us looking for God to swoop down and remove the source of whatever fear we're facing. Through the conflict and resolution of both Elijah's and the Cowardly Lion's dilemma, we learn that our fears need to be faced head-on. No amount of running away will enable us to overcome. Scripture tells us we have an enemy who is relentless, an enemy who will not stop until he is made to stop.

> *The thief comes only to steal, kill and destroy.*
> *(John 10:10)*

Nothing would please the devil more than to steal or destroy the confidence with which God has equipped each of His children. The most effective way for him to do that is to separate us from one another. When the only voice we're hearing is the voice of the enemy telling us "it's no use; you're incapable" or "you're just not strong enough to make it," it's easy to have our confidence and our courage shaken. The most effective route for us to take at times such as these is to run, not walk, into the arms of God our Jehovah-Jireh (the One who provides).

Chances are, He will provide alright; He'll more than likely provide for someone to come alongside us, someone who is obedient to His calling, and pour into us a measure of His courage through words of inspiration and validation. Don't ever dismiss a word of encouragement coming from any source without at least considering it being a word from the Lord. Some of the most profound inspirations in my life have come from the least likely sources. Remember, God can and will use whatever and whomever He chooses.

### Assume the role of encourager

Do you know any Cowardly Lions in your life? Most of us do. Instead of allowing them to walk around anxious and fearful with their tails between their legs, worrying about everything under the sun, why not assume the role of encourager and help restore their confidence. It will likely take only a few choice words of encouragement to remind them of the times you have witnessed their courage in the past. Telling them how their strength of character has been an inspiration to you can only work to enhance their self-esteem and demonstrate to them this fear they're experiencing need only be temporary.

And if that Cowardly Lion happens to be you, simply let the Word of God remind you where your strength comes from. Listen attentively as God reminds you of the number of times He has already enabled you to overcome. Don't allow this transient fear of the moment to overshadow the power and the courage that is living and breathing inside of you.

> *For God did not give us a spirit of timidity,*
> *but a spirit of power.*
> *(2 Timothy 1:7)*

Maybe what you're experiencing isn't a lack of courage at all; maybe it's just the universal need we all have from time to time of being reassured by our Heavenly Father that He's still completely in charge. That assurance is but a Scripture verse away as well.

> *God has said, never will I leave you;*
> *never will I forsake you.*
> *(Hebrews 13:5)*

Now that's something no Wizard could ever make good on.

**Remember...**
- Encouragement is the act of supplying courage to someone else by way of doing something or saying something that inspires them.
- God has given each of His children ample courage to overcome any and all fear.
- Don't dismiss the idea that your most recent encouragement, even though it came from a friend, didn't originate from God.

*Take a lesson from the Wizard*

Challenge yourself to see how many "medals of encouragement" you can go around hanging on the chests of the fearful. Pray for opportunities to restore the courage in others by simply reminding them what God has provided is more than sufficient. If there have been times when they inspired you with their courage, share it with them. I have a feeling they'll be ready to stand up to any "wicked witch" after you've validated them with your words of encouragement.

# 2

# The Concept Behind Encouragement

*But encourage one another daily as long as it is called today.*
*(Hebrews 3:13)*

Encouragement. What an amazing concept. I say something to you that inspires you and makes you feel good about who you are, and then you in turn say something to someone else that inspires them and makes them feel good about who they are. And before you know it, there are people all around who are more confident and more secure, and who walk with a little more bounce in their step then they ever did before. Encouragement really is a remarkable thing. It takes very little effort, there's an endless supply of it, and its results can be life-changing. Not bad for something that also happens to be free.

It's not difficult to understand why encouragement is so remarkable; it's a concept created by God. Not only has God designed it, making it flawless, but also He has given each of us the ability and the opportunity to put His encouragement into action daily. To think that every one of us holds the key to enable others to improve their attitude, their outlook, and their self-esteem is something most of us rarely, if ever, think about. It's either we don't think about it, or the majority of us are so busy worrying about getting our own needs met that we have no time left to encourage others. Either way it's inexcusable. There's a whole world of people out there who could benefit greatly from nothing more than an encouraging word, people whose lives could be positively impacted by our merely affirming them.

**The best part is …it's so simple**

It devastates me when I hear people say they feel as though their lives have little or no meaning, that they see no real purpose for their existence. Somewhere along the line, they were deceived into believing they don't make a difference. Often that deception is triggered by someone close to them, someone it should never come from, someone such as a parent or a spouse. It's so easy to lose heart and give up when all you hear are words of despair and discouragement, and believe me there are plenty of people out there hearing a lot of despair and discouragement.

One of the objectives in writing this book was to get people to see themselves as God sees them, because the truth is, to Him every life has great purpose and incredible meaning. That godly meaning and purpose for our lives is never made more evident than when we begin to positively impact the lives of others. God has given each of us the potential to play a significant role in others' lives, and our significance can be fully appreciated when we become people of encouragement.

By using this God-given gift, we begin to discover our full potential as encouraging vessels for God. If you desire more meaning to your life, then begin consciously encouraging and affirming others; by doing so, you will undoubtedly discover an incredible meaning you never knew existed. I challenge you to see not just how much you can change the emotional climate of where you live, but how you can demonstrate for others the true character of God. Chances are, as you begin noticing a considerable difference in the attitude of those around you, your life and your purpose in life will become much more significant.

The best part of becoming an encourager is how simple it is. You don't have to plan out what you're going to say, you don't have to wait for the ideal moment, and contrary to what you may think, you don't have to be an etymologist (that's a person who studies words; I looked it up). Too often people hesitate in encouraging others because they feel as though they don't know what words to say. In all reality, that is the least significant aspect in you becoming a person of encouragement. People appreciate much more the fact that you desire to validate them than they do about what words you choose to validate them. Really, it's true.

Let me ask you, when you receive a greeting card, whether it's a birthday card, a get well card, or some made-up holiday card, and you aren't sure who the card is from, what's the first thing you do when you open it? Do you read the little verse inside or do you first sneak a peek to see who sent you the card? If you work for Hallmark, you might read the entire card first, but if you're like me, the moment you open the card your eyes scan down to the name at the bottom. That's because the act itself is more important to us than the things that constitute the act. In all sincerity, when it comes down to encouraging other people, words can be grossly overrated.

**Most contagious of all human behaviors**
The best part of becoming an encourager may be how simple it is, but the easiest part of encouraging others is getting people to appreciate your encouragement. We can thank God for that. You see, He has created each one of us with the desire to be encouraged. And while being encouraged is one of the most sought after of all human desires, it's also one of the least experienced. I have yet to meet the person who doesn't welcome a verbal *pat on the back* from time to time. As a matter of fact, the vast majority of people enthusiastically welcome encouragement from others. Their inexperience in being encouraged might cause them to feel a little unsettled at first, but they'll quickly get over that.

Hearing someone encourage you just makes you feel good, and since we all like to feel good, we can't help but respond positively to others' words of affirmation. If you're unsure what it is that constitutes encouragement, just put yourself in their place, and think how you would feel if a friend walked up to you and said something like: "I really admire how you always seem so positive; I wish I could be more like you."

That's all I'm talking about, telling people things that will inspire them and cause them to see themselves as they were created to be, people with purpose and meaning. Maybe you have never looked at yourself as a potential encourager, thinking maybe it's not part of your personality. Don't accept that. First of all, you're obviously selling yourself short, and, second, just because you've never been a conscious encourager before doesn't mean you can't start now.

I'm fifty-nine, and I began my quest to consciously encourage those around me about two years ago. And while I can't witness as to the difference it's made in their lives, I can tell you the difference it's made in my life has been more than significant. I now see another purpose for my life. That purpose is found in knowing I can make a difference in the lives of others, a significant difference.

Can you become an encourager? Surely you can; and as you begin transforming into that person others look to for inspiration, don't be surprised at how much others begin encouraging you. I have found encouraging to be one of the most contagious of all human behaviors. One person can affect a whole population. One person who is willing to love others enough to step out of his or her comfort zone and begin shining God's light into the hearts of those around him can cause an epidemic of encouragement. Perhaps that someone is you. Now I know what some of you are thinking. "Me! Oh, that can never be me; I'm just not like that. You want me to pray for people fine, but to actually engage them in conversation and speak words that affirm them, well, that's just not me."

Who told you that? I'm serious. Who was it that walked up to you after evaluating your life and told you, "You could never be a person of encouragement"? Chances are, no one has ever done that, but even if someone did tell you that, who are they to say such a thing?

"Well, Reid, I just know myself too well. Some people can do that; I'm just not one of them." Let me ask you: Have you always been able to drive a car? I mean when you were, let's say four years old, could you drive a car? No, you couldn't. You had to learn. You practiced and you learned. If you were like my children, there were times I wasn't convinced they would ever learn, but they did, and so did you. My point is, maybe encouraging others isn't something you have ever done; maybe the thought of going around telling others positive things about themselves frightens you. Just remember this, encouraging is something God has called us all to do; and when God calls us, God enables us. Do you trust Him enough to be your enabler? If you do, you have to get your eyes off the limits of your abilities and begin to look to the limitless abilities of God.

*Now to him who is able to do immeasurably more than all we ask or imagine, according to his power that is at work within us.*
*(Ephesians 3:20)*

### Remember...
- Being encouraged is one of the most sought after of all human desires.
- Each of us holds the key of enabling others to improve their attitude, their outlook, and their self-esteem; that key is the act of encouraging.
- Becoming an encourager will give you newfound significance for your life.

### Anyone can do it
It's easy to sit on the sidelines of life and watch others take chances. One of the problems with that attitude, however, is it will never allow you to experience the thrill and satisfaction of participating. I have discovered

that few things in life give you the thrill or the satisfaction found in being an encourager. Putting a heartfelt smile on someone's face is a gift that blesses in both directions. You see, God fashioned encouragement to bless the life of the one receiving it as well as the one giving it. Add to that the fact that when we participate in encouraging, God is honored. Regardless of who you are, it's never too late to start. That's the one thing about the concepts of God; age and time are irrelevant.

# 3

# Why and How
# Encouragement Works

*May our Lord Jesus Christ himself and God our Father, who
loved us and by his grace gave us eternal encouragement and
good hope, encourage your hearts and strengthen you in every
good deed and word.*
*(2 Thessalonians 2:16-17)*

The reason encouragement works is because it's from God. It's was
His idea. Being the omniscient God that He is, He knows how it
makes us feel when we're encouraged. He's fully aware of the discourage-
ment the enemy uses to beat people down. Fear, stress, worry, panic, anx-
iety, and apprehension are all tools the devil uses in his attempt to keep us
bound. God knows encouragement works to release those who are spiritu-
ally and emotionally bound; it's the reason He created it. Encouragement
isn't something man thought of on his own; it has much deeper roots. For
us to truly understand God's concept of encouragement, we have to go
back to the very beginning.

### Eve was to be a full partner
In the beginning, God walked with man and He talked with man. In the
beginning, God shared His garden with man; man and God co-existed. The
experience of that relationship could not have been anything but amazing.
Imagine how confident and secure you would feel knowing you were cre-
ated in the image of God and then spending the afternoon with Him. How

encouraging would it have been to wake up every day and know you had the undivided attention of the One who hung the stars in place?

That relationship between man and God continued to develop right up until the time God had given to Adam everything He had created. One can only envision the beauty and enormity of what God had entrusted to man, which, when you think of it, was a way of encouraging him even further. Can you picture in your mind the look on Adam's face when his Creator scanned the entire garden and said He was placing him in charge of it all? We're not sure of everything the garden contained, but included in all the remarkable things growing there was more than enough to sustain man.

*Then God said, "I give you every seed-bearing plant on the face*
*of the whole earth and every tree that has fruit with seed in it.*
*They will be yours for food."*
*(Genesis 1:29)*

Man then learned that with possession comes responsibility.

*You are free to eat from any tree in the garden; but you must*
*not eat from the tree of the knowledge of good and evil.*
*(Genesis 2:16-17)*

Adam was soon to realize the garden was just the tip of the iceberg. God was about to encourage his socks off!

*The Lord God said, "It is not good for the man to be alone.*
*I will make a helper suitable for him."*
*(Genesis 2:18)*

When God gave Eve to Adam, He demonstrated just how much He loved him. I'm sure Paradise would have been pretty awesome had Adam experienced it by himself, but when he was given someone else to share it with, his joy was doubled; and for that matter, so was Eve's. You see, Eve was to be a full partner in this relationship. This word *helper* means, among other things, "counterpart." Eve was never to be a subordinate of Adam, as though she was in some way inferior to him. She was to help, or enhance, Adam's experience on this earth; just as Adam was to help, or enhance, Eve's experience equally as well.

One way they were to help one another was to be fruitful and propagate their kind upon the land. That obviously couldn't happen without either Adam or Eve. But propagating wasn't their only responsibility; they also had the responsibility of being one another's friend. The truth is, God could not have encouraged Adam any more than by giving him a friend. I've come across many definitions for the word *friend*, but here's my all-time favorite:

> *Friend: "Someone who enhances another's life*
> *by unconditionally fulfilling the needs they have."*

**God never stops loving us**
You see, before we call ourselves somebody's friend, we should be taking inventory of what needs they have and evaluating how well we're fulfilling them. One of the most profound ways of fulfilling needs in others' lives is through encouragement. Look again at the story of Eden. Right after God encouraged Adam by first endowing everything to him, He then created Eve and bound the two to one another. Now we all know what happened after that. They ate from the forbidden tree and God cast them from His physical presence. Talk about going from the penthouse to the outhouse!

Now, as a result of the Fall, I would have to believe the young couple had to be going through what amounted to a great deal of shame and remorse. Once privy to everything God had created, they now found themselves on the outside looking in. Having lost pretty much everything God was willing to bequeath to them, they found themselves in need. Their greatest need, of course, was the grace of God; but apart from grace, can you think of their next greatest need? If you were to ask me, I would tell you, emphatically, it was encouragement.

You have to understand something here. Adam and Eve went from daily walking and conversing with God to being totally cut off, overnight. With man now removed from God's presence, it meant, among so many other things, Adam would no longer be on the receiving end of God's words of affirmation. Man's daily dose of inspiration from the lips of Yahwch Himself would never again be heard in the ears of Adam. It's difficult to put yourself in Adam's place because no one else has ever experienced such an exclusive alliance with God. To lose that relationship is obviously unparalleled.

What an immediate and insurmountable void that had to create. God, the Creator and Sustainer of the Universe, goes from being your best friend to locking you out of His presence. That cannot be an easy thing to imagine. Adam and Eve literally went from having *it all* to having *nothing*;

nothing except one another, that is. God was still the Creator and Sustainer of their lives alright; He just wasn't going to be their friend as they once knew Him to be. That void of friend (and encourager) to man, was now going to have to be fulfilled, that's right, by man himself. Remember our earlier definition of *friend*:

> *"Someone who enhances the life of someone else*
> *by unconditionally fulfilling the needs they have."*

In the beginning, that Someone was God fulfilling those needs; first-hand. After the Fall, with man and God's relationship taking such a severe hit, God could no longer encourage His creation face-to-face. Now, before I go on, there's one thing I want to make clear about what Adam and Eve's actions *didn't* do. While God may have expelled the couple from His presence, He never stopped loving them. I should say, He never stopped loving them unconditionally.

God was, God is, and God will forever be our Father regardless of whether or not we always choose to do what He says. Unconditional love is just that; it's *unconditional*. Choosing to love us despite our failings is the definition of His love. While God doesn't need to ever prove His love to us, He all but did by giving to us the gift of one another. God may no longer walk and talk with us in the same manner He did with Adam and Eve, by encouraging us face to face. He can, however, use us, His children, to carry on His work as one another's encourager. Every one of us has been given the ability to fulfill His role of face-to-face encourager. We can't be God, obviously, but certainly we can demonstrate, at least in part, His love to one another.

> *Your attitude should be the same as that of Christ Jesus.*
> *(Philippians 2:5)*

One of the most powerful ways of demonstrating God's love is to come alongside someone who is hurting and be Christ to them. That shouldn't be too difficult since God saw to it to place the Spirit of the living Christ in all who ask.

> *Do you not realize that Christ Jesus is in you.*
> *(2 Corinthians 13:5)*

**Being loved is a desire of all God's children**

True, Adam and Eve no longer shared the intimacy with God they once had, but they were given one another to share intimacy. The intimacy they shared, more than likely included encouragement. The love of God is loaded with encouragement, and when we demonstrate His love to our spouses, our co-workers, our family, and our friends, we are fulfilling a need mankind has had from the beginning of time.

There isn't a person living or dead who hasn't needed or appreciated encouragement from time to time. And since our sin is what's responsible for us no longer walking hand in hand with God in the garden, hearing Him audibly speak words of encouragement to us, it's our responsibility and privilege to model this love of the Father to one another. The best part is, we can do it in so many different ways. Let's turn again to Scripture for an example. There is nothing else in all of God's Word that speaks more loudly to man's need for encouragement than Matthew 3:17, where we read about the baptism of Jesus. When Christ arose out of the water and heaven was opened, and the Holy Spirit descended on Him like a dove, do you recall what His Heavenly Father said?

> *And a voice from heaven said, "This is my Son,*
> *whom I love; with him I am well pleased."*

This account from Scripture, which served to launch the earthly ministry of our Lord, demonstrates two important aspects of encouragement. First, it demonstrates that a son is entitled to receive his father's blessing (obviously it's not limited to male children or to fathers). It also demonstrates a father's awareness of the importance of *verbally* encouraging his son. I'm sure God could have spoken into Jesus' spirit all kinds of encouragement, but He chose instead to verbally praise Him. I have to believe God did so to demonstrate to us the importance of others hearing our words of affirmation. It's one thing to believe others want us to be encouraged, but it's something else altogether to audibly hear those words that lift our spirits.

Now let's look at *how* God encouraged Jesus. He started by telling Him that He loved Him. This is a much overlooked need and under-practiced deed. Being loved is an intrinsic desire of all God's children. Again, while we may assume we're loved, to actually hear the words is a tremendous source of encouragement. Telling someone you love that you love them never gets old. Jesus was also validated by His Heavenly Father when He (the Father) said how *"well pleased"* He was with His Son. We can never hear too much of that! When someone tells us they're pleased with us, our self-esteem goes through the roof. To think our relationship with another person is for them a source of joy, our sense of worth skyrockets. The Father's encouragement for His Son that day in Galilee had to be an incredible source of encouragement for Jesus as He began His three and a half years of portraying His Father to the world.

### Don't wait for a reason

It's also interesting to note that the Father said He was well-pleased with His Son *prior* to His Son's ministry. Jesus hadn't healed any lepers or filled even one water glass with wine, yet His Father was still well-pleased with Him. What a lesson! God demonstrates to us (also His sons and daughters) through this account of Scripture that it's not in the things we do for Him that causes Him to be well-pleased. He's well-pleased with us for simply being His son or His daughter. God is saying, "I love you and I'm well-pleased with you because I have created you as the person you are," *period.*

Now this may be hard for us to understand, but that's because we don't comprehend unconditional love. Our relationships on earth are based mostly on what I can do for you and what you can do for me. Thankfully that's not how God deals with us; and we can learn a lot by modeling our Heavenly Father's example. Now, how can we take this real-life account from biblical history and assimilate it into our lives? It's simple; don't wait for your daughter to bring home all A's on her report card before telling her how well-pleased you are with her. Let your husband know you're well-pleased with him before he paints the guest room or cleans the gutters. Inform your employees just how much you appreciate them prior to them nailing the big account.

It's so obvious that God doesn't tie "things" to His affirmations and encouragement, and because He doesn't, neither should we. Think about this: If God the Father took the time to demonstrate the importance of encouraging His Son Jesus, then why do you suppose we fail so often to encourage those we love and care for? I believe you'll discover the reasons why as you move through this book. I also believe you'll discover, along the way, how essential your words of affirmation become in transforming the lives of those around you. Just be ready; because it's impossible to become a person of encouragement without your own life experiencing a radical but amazing transformation as well.

***Remember...***
- God knows encouragement works to release those who are spiritually and emotionally bound; it's the reason He created it.
- God could not have encouraged Adam any more than by giving him a friend.
- One of the most powerful ways of demonstrating God's love is to come alongside someone who is hurting and be Christ to them.

### *You can be God's mouthpiece*

We know that God no longer speaks to us as He did with Adam, but since God doesn't love us one ounce less than He did Adam, He designed a way to continue communicating and encouraging us. And He does it by using us. If you'll take the time to listen to God, I can assure you He will prompt you to speak words of encouragement to others. The more often we listen and the more often we obey, the more often God will use us. Become God's mouthpiece; love those around you by offering to them the Father's words of nourishment and life.

# 4

# The Selfish Truth About Encouragement

*If you harbor...selfish ambition in your hearts,*
*do not boast about it or deny the truth.*
*(James 3:14)*

The truth about encouragement is, everyone appreciates receiving it whether they admit it or not. Some people tend to react as though they could take it or leave it, but that has more to do with not knowing how to respond to someone's encouragement than it does with not desiring to hear it. As I mentioned earlier, being encouraged fulfills a desire we all have, the desire to be validated by others.

All of us want to be reassured that we are basically good people who are making a positive contribution to society, but unless someone in that society lets us know our contribution is positive, we're left on our own to speculate. This uncertainty of our worth contributes to the apprehensive self-doubting attitude far too many of us live with. That's why encouragement is so essential; it not only dispels our doubt, it also inspires much needed confidence.

If we can get introspective for a moment and examine our subconscious motives, we're going to discover that we're all pretty insecure people. Not only are we insecure, but also we're pretty self-centered. When those two qualities are combined, it results in us not only desiring but *needing* the validation of others. It's not really our fault that we are like this; we come by it naturally, and it begins revealing itself when we're quite young. As children, we're constantly asking Mom or Dad for positive feedback to reinforce how we're doing.

The two-year-old holds up a picture she has just drawn and asks, *"This is pretty, isn't it, Mommy?"*

The little boy returning home with his father from his T-ball game wants to be reassured. *"Daddy, did I hit the ball good today?"*

I can't tell you how many times I heard my own children ask their mother when they were little, *"Mom, are you sure we're gonna look like you and not Daddy when we grow up?"*

That desire to be reassured and validated doesn't weaken when we're older. We may not come right out and ask our boss, "Hey, Mr. Jennings, did I do a good job today?" But if Mr. Jennings happens to say you did a good job today, tomorrow you're coming to work with a little different attitude. That's what I don't understand; if encouraging my employees will cause them to take a little more pride in their work, or encouraging my students will inspire them to study more diligently, then why oh why aren't more of us utilizing this God-given resource? Not only will encouragement work on motivating us to increase productivity, it also satisfies a physiological need all people have.

*You see, in the mid-sagittal section of the human brain just slightly above the brain stem, a variety of synapses are constantly processing stimuli and sending them via receptors to neighboring neurons. In humans, a certain chemical substance called dopamine, known to reduce anxiety and at the same time satisfy certain desires the body has, is produced. One of those desires is to be stroked, reinforced, or validated. When people receive encouragement, brain activity increases in the sagittal area, sending increased amounts of dopamine to our neurotransmitters, which then tell the brain that all is well. This, in turn, produces confidence in one's self, thus boosting one's self esteem. Amazing how all that works, isn't it?*

To be perfectly honest, everything you just read in that last paragraph is nonsense. I know, because I made it all up. I have no idea what a neurotransmitter does. It did sound pretty impressive though, didn't it? And I'm willing to bet if all that information was somehow proven through science, the majority of you would be nodding your collective heads as if to say, "Yeah, that makes sense." Well, if believing all of that helps convince you that encouragement boosts self-esteem, then be my guest.

The truth is, I didn't make it *all* up. There is a mid-sagittal section of the brain alright, but I couldn't tell you for the life of me what goes on there. It's not even important; the only thing you have to know when it comes to encouraging someone is that it truly does make them feel better. Chemical substances being released or not, when you affirm another person, they will one-hundred percent of the time walk away from you with a smile on their face and a song in their heart. OK, maybe the song in their heart is pushing it a bit, but what's wrong with just making someone smile? Lord knows, we could use a few more smiling people these days. The fact that there may not be any neurological enhancement from being encouraged should not, in the least bit, stop you from practicing it. I may not be able to tell you what, if any, physiological benefit is derived from receiving encouragement, but I can tell you there is plenty of emotional benefit. I conducted my own unofficial poll and asked forty-seven people this question:

*If someone were to walk up to you and speak encouragement over you, would you:*

A. *Feel better about yourself,*
B. *Feel worse about yourself or*
C. *Feel nothing?*

The result was forty-seven A's. See there, and we don't need any medical evidence to back this up. Go ahead, conduct your own poll and discover for yourself how the overwhelming majority of people feel about being encouraged. I'm betting your results won't be any different from mine. So then, the question remains, why aren't more of us handing out encouragement? It astounds me really. The ability to empower and affirm others is right there on the tip of our tongues, yet we refuse to allow the words to go forth as if we're waiting for the Surgeon General to declare "Encouragement is not hazardous to our health." Why is that? Why do we find it so difficult to speak life or health into another human being when the only downside to us is… ah… well… come to think of it, there is no downside to us. So, if that's the case, if the cost of encouraging someone is zilch, if the effort to encourage is negligible, then why in the world are there so many people we know walking around discouraged, depressed and defeated?

The answer to that question is both simple and, at the same time, troubling. The truth is, those of us who are able to do something about it, aren't. The theory behind encouraging others is not only sound, it's perfect, but unless it's put into action, it remains nothing but a theory. If you haven't noticed, God isn't real big on theorizing. He's more a fan of application.

*Faith by itself, if it is not accompanied by action, is dead.*
*(James 2:17)*

**Filling the cups of others**

The Word of God constantly encourages its readers to take action. Christianity hasn't prospered for two-thousand years because its followers love to speculate and hypothesize; Christianity has prospered because its followers have faithfully and boldly lived out their convictions. Encouraging others is faithfully living out our convictions. Paul's letters to the First Century churches are loaded with the call to encourage one another. Even Paul, whose faith could never be brought into question, had one main longing as he desired to visit the young Christians in those churches.

*I long to see you…that you and I may be*
*mutually encouraged by each other's faith.*
*(Romans 1:11-12)*

God foreknew Paul's need to be supported and inspired. I'm sure that's why He provided him with the young companion Barnabas, whose name actually means "son of encouragement." Don't ever think God was caught by surprise at the continuous struggle His followers would experience as they persevered through great odds in establishing His church. As the omniscient eternal God that He is, He made provision to counter the world's oppression against His people by endowing each of us with the ability to encourage one other. Don't think just because your name isn't Barnabas you can't be a *child of encouragement*; and don't think that the First Century believers were the only ones who needed to be encouraged. Look around you for goodness sake; does it look as though this world is a model for Christ's Church? If there's anything God's people need today, it's encouragement.

The concept of encouraging others is biblical, therefore it's flawless. There's only one problem relative to encouragement. It must be put into effect by less than flawless people, people whose nature is much more akin to selfishness than it is to sacrifice. Encouraging others requires us to put on hold our desire to be stroked in lieu of stroking others. That's why I believe there's such a shortage of true encouragers today.

It has become the philosophy of so many, even those within the Church, to get our own cups filled before we go about filling the cups of others. The problem with that philosophy, outside of the fact that it's unscriptural, is that once we discover how much pleasure our flesh gains in having our cups filled, filling the cups of others begins to hold less and less significance. Encouragement consists in filling the cups of others, but when that desire becomes eleventh on our top ten list of things to do each day, it's easy to see why so many around us go unencouraged.

It really boils down to one thing: selfishness. I wish I could say it didn't. I wish I could use another word to describe it, but I can't. I can't because selfish is exactly what it is. The ugly truth is, people are inherently selfish; it's part of our fleshly makeup; has been from the start. Little children never need lessons on how to hoard their toys or how not to share their food. Sharing our things is a practice that needs constant practice. The same holds true for our attitudes about encouraging.

Encouraging can be seen as verbally sharing our toys. Have you ever observed little children at play? If a child shares his or her toy with a friend and that friend begins having too much fun with that toy, watch what happens. The child who loaned the toy wants it back. He wants it back because the friend is having a lot more fun with that toy than he ever did. I think most of us understand little children haven't developed the skills or the discipline it takes to put their desires on hold in an effort to meet the desires of others. I also believe we'd all be surprised to know how many adults are still of that undisciplined childish mindset when it comes to sharing encouragement. In the back of our minds we're thinking: "If I start handing out too much encouragement, then all those people I encourage might begin to feel a whole lot better about themselves than I do about myself. As a matter of fact, they might even begin enjoying their lives way more than I'm enjoying my life. And I can't have that."

When people have no spiritual foundation for their lives, everything is centered on self. Self is first, self is last, and self is pretty much everything in between. When self is first and foremost, it almost always means encouraging others has to take a backseat, because everything up here in the front seat deals with me. What a lonely and unfulfilled life that must be.

As long as I'm working the pulpit here, there's something else that needs to be said. I've discovered there are people who don't encourage others because, quite frankly, they're miserable people. Most of the time they choose to be miserable, and just as misery loves company, their desire is for others to be as despondent as they are. Somehow they've come to adopt a distorted philosophy that says as long as there are others walking around as sad and depressed as they are, then they can feel better about themselves; as though there's some kind of comfort in sharing misery. So out of the fear of having to face despair all alone, they avoid encouraging others in a desperate attempt to keep themselves from being the only miserable person around. Their greatest fear is that there won't be anyone left to wallow with in their misery. If you ask me, you can't get much more selfish than that.

**Selfishness has to be broken**

I think most people would agree that selfishness is a trait that comes to us quite naturally, one that constantly looks to be fed and reinforced. To prove it, all we'd need to do is follow someone around who we know to be gloomy and miserable, and write down all the instances where they went out of their way to encourage someone else. Chances are we wouldn't have to bother bringing paper or pencil.

The lie and deception of selfishness tells us our lives will somehow lose worth if someone else's life becomes more enriched. So obviously those who have bought into that line of thinking aren't going to initiate any type of encouragement themselves. The devil has become rather adept at keeping the truth about encouragement from being revealed. It's obvious to the vast majority of us that if we help lift someone out of their misery, we're going to feel better about ourselves as well.

The thought of knowing we've impacted the life of someone else in a positive way is only going to work to enhance our own self-concept. That is the truth. I don't care how hardened or dour a person is, if they do something (even inadvertently) to enrich another person's life, they're going to feel better about themselves. Even if they don't want to feel better, there's no way of getting around it, because feeling better is a natural sensation all humans experience following the act of encouraging. Getting them to admit it might be a little difficult, but that doesn't change the fact that they still experienced a feeling of well-being.

On the other hand, if all they do is go around wrapped up in their own selfish little lonely world doing nothing to help lift anyone else out of their misery, it's a pretty safe bet they're never going to feel better about themselves. Misery perpetuates misery. It's nothing short of the spiritual bondage of selfishness, and it has to be broken. One way to help break the bond of selfishness is to practice encouragement. If you're the one who tends to be a bit selfish, speak one or two words of encouragement to someone else and see for yourself how it makes you feel. If you're into making yourself feel good, here is a great way of doing it without being selfish. Attempting to break someone else of their selfishness however is a bit more complicated; it's going to take persistence and it's going to take patience. It's really a case of wearing them down with kindness, which, by the way, is another excellent way of making oneself feel good without being selfish.

> *A kind man benefits himself.*
> *(Proverbs 11:17)*

None of this stuff is new; the apostle Paul preached it to the church in Philippi two-thousand years ago.

> *Do nothing out of selfish ambition...*
> *but in humility consider others better than yourselves.*
> *(Philippians 2:3)*

That's not an easy Scripture verse. It's easy to read, yes; it's just not easy to live. We are called to consider others better than we consider ourselves. Did you see that? Let me have you read it again, this time with a little more emphasis. **We** (that's you and I) are **called** (mandated by God Himself) to consider **others** (everyone else) **better** (in a more superior way) than we consider ourselves! And while this is only possible through the enablement of God, when we actually get to that place, our lives begin to experience some amazing things. When we begin making the effort to see the needs of others and then look to fulfill those needs, when serving self no longer becomes our first and only daily concern, guess what? We discover rather quickly that our own needs and desires get met in the process. Don't ask me to explain how that happens. I just know it does. It's the power of God's Word coming to fruition. Follow His Word obediently and He will provide.

> *But seek first his kingdom and his righteousness,*
> *and all these things will be given to you as well.*
> *(Matthew 6:33)*

Whether our refusal to encourage others is due to selfishness or being in the possession of a miserable attitude really doesn't matter. What matters is the moment we begin following the Word of God and encouraging others, two incredible things take place. Not only will we see others experience purpose in their lives, but an amazing purpose will saturate our lives as well. And this purpose has the potential to replace all misery and self-ishness we've permitted to rob us of the joy and contentment God desires us to possess. We can experience the grief and agony of practicing misery and selfishness or the joy and contentment found from encouraging others. The choice, as always, is ours.

### *Remember…*

- The only thing you have to know when it comes to encouraging someone is that it truly does make them feel better.
- Everyone appreciates receiving encouragement whether they admit it or not.
- Encouraging others requires us to put on hold our desire to be stroked in lieu of stroking others.

### *Time to trade in our selfishness*

Those of us in the body of Christ truly know better. We've read and we've heard how selfishness cannot be allowed to dwell in the lives of believers. We also know what a constant battle it is to rid our lives of such a harassing spirit. I suggest we stop battling it. Fighting against it hasn't made a significant difference in our lives up to now, has it? I mean, is there ever a day we don't get selfish thoughts or carry out selfish action? So here's what I propose: Instead of fighting the urge to be selfish, let's just replace it with the practice of encouraging others. Let's just trade in, so to speak; our selfish thoughts and actions for God's desire to uplift and inspire those around us. This way we're actually living out two of God's principles for our lives simultaneously. We're blessing others and ignoring the temptation to be selfish.

5

# Becoming the Encouragee

*Your enthusiasm has stirred them to action.*
*(2 Corinthians 9:2)*

**En-courag-ee**; *in-ker-ij-ee. Noun. A person who receives encouragement*
*with* **enthusiasm** *and a thankful* **heart.**

I recently became the recipient of a great deal of encouragement. The
means for receiving it, however, wasn't particularly enjoyable. Three
weeks before I began to write this book, my orthopedic surgeon, Doctor
Robert Piston, cut an eight-inch incision through the muscle of my left
hip, dislocated the femoral head from its socket, and took a surgical saw
and lopped off the top of my femur. He then proceeded to drill down six
inches into the core of my femur and pound (no less than twenty times)
a manufactured rod made of cobalt and chrome into the bored-out hole.
He followed that by again drilling and then attaching a prosthetic cup
into my pelvis. After connecting a metal ball onto the rod, he snapped the
two pieces together and sewed me up. Seven days post-op, I was walking
around, without assistance, with a brand new hip; it was an amazing thing.

Now there is a reason for me telling you all that; granted it could have
been a little less graphic, but I wanted you to think of this from my perspec-
tive. My wife would say I also wanted to get your sympathy since I'm such
a baby when it comes to pain. She knows me all too well. Furthermore I
wanted you to know, as a result of my surgery, I had people coming out of
the woodwork to encourage me.

The hospital employees encouraged me while I recovered from sur-
gery, the rehab people picked up where the hospital employees left off, and

once I arrived home, friends, family and members of my church combined to affirm and assist me through a couple of rough weeks. As I became overwhelmed by all their support and efforts to encourage me through my recovery, it caused me to become glaringly aware of something I discovered to be a much overlooked, yet extremely significant, aspect of encouragement. As the target of so many inspiring words, I was made conscious of just how important the attitude is of the person receiving the encouragement.

I can't believe I've never thought of this before, especially since I have been the recipient of so much encouragement in my life. It's probably because I have never broken it down and examined it to such a degree. I had always been under the impression that encouragement was comprised of someone saying something nice to someone else and that was pretty much it. But after this in-depth study, coupled with the recent experiences I went through during the recovery from my surgery, I must admit there's more to it than that. A whole lot more.

I have discovered it takes the cooperation of no less than two people before encouragement can achieve all that God desires it to achieve. Obviously there must be the one who sends the encouragement, the encourager, but in addition to that, there must be the one who receives that encouragement, the encouragee. Both the encourager and the encouragee must work together in order for the words sent to affirm can do so. I'm willing to bet most of you have never realized this before; I know I hadn't. You see, the encouragee's role is every bit as essential as the encourager's in determining whether or not any and all encouragement achieves its purpose.

**The pass has to be completed**

Let me give you a football analogy to explain what I mean. Let's say a football team has a great quarterback; he can throw every type of pass there is. The thirty-yard out isn't a problem, the soft touch over the corner's head is perfected, and no one can zing it between two linebackers like this guy. Leaving his hand, the football is a thing of beauty; the problem can develop, however, when it arrives at the receiver's hands. The ball goes where it's intended but the receiver is all thumbs. The ball bounces off his chest, or it goes right through his hands; either way it ends up on the ground as incomplete.

When the quarterback threw the pass, it started out with great potential; however it became ineffective due to the receiver's inability to *welcome* the ball into his possession. Even though it was a great pass, it was ruled unsuccessful since the receiver never took ownership of the ball. In other words, the receiver never validated his quarterback. If there is something that will frustrate a quarterback and cause him to stop throwing passes in a receiver's direction, it's a receiver who doesn't validate his passes. Quarterbacks need to be validated, and when they're not, it's only a matter of time before they start taking their passes elsewhere.

I see a great correlation between a quarterback and his receiver, and the encourager and his encouragee. When encouragement leaves the mouth of the encourager, just like the quarterback's pass, it carries with it great potential. Among other things, it can energize a person's spirit or brighten a person's day. In addition to fulfilling any number of needs the encouragee may have, it also carries the potential to validate the encourager as well. There's no small amount of satisfaction one receives from knowing he has enhanced the life of someone else. In order for encouragement to realize its potential, it must complete its mission. In other words, there must be a reception of that encouragement by the encouragee. If our encouragement is not welcomed, if it is not received, there can be no satisfaction experienced by either party. Just as a quarterback cannot receive satisfaction if his passes get dropped, an encourager cannot experience any fulfillment if his words go unreceived.

There is one main difference though between a passing play in football and encouraging others in life. In life, all of us get to play both receiver and quarterback. There are times we're going to encourage others and times others are going to encourage us. If we only excel in one of those areas and not the other, it correlates to having a team of good quarterbacks throwing to a bunch of bad receivers. The result of that combination can rarely, if ever, be good.

**Our response is the key**

God has placed within each one of us the desire to be encouraged; to deny that desire is telling God He really doesn't know what He's doing. Encouraging others, when done sincerely, will actually fulfill that God-given desire in both the giver and the receiver. For many people, responding appropriately to the encouragement of others doesn't come naturally; it may take a little work.

The truth is, receiving encouragement can be a little uncomfortable for anyone, and for a number of reasons. For example, when people compliment or affirm us, there's a good chance it catches us off guard. We can blame that on the infrequency with which most people are encouraged. Our face may get flush or we find ourselves stumbling around for something to say. It's not uncommon for false humility to take over and cause us to say something humorous in an attempt to move on. Unfortunately, what is even more prevalent is us dismissing the person's remarks as unnecessary. That's a mistake. When we dismiss an encouraging word given to us as unnecessary, or we pretend to make light of it, we are robbing the encourager of a blessing.

Encouragement is a gift, and when we dismiss it as unnecessary, what we're really doing is turning our backs on this very personal present all wrapped up with our name on it. How would you feel if you thought you picked out the perfect gift and when you tried to give it to the person it was intended for, they said, "No thanks"?

I don't remember the first time I heard someone say, "It is more blessed to give than to receive," but growing up I never fully bought into it. I don't think many little children do. It isn't until we've grown up a bit that its significance becomes reality and it's then we discover for ourselves the fulfillment found in giving. Giving to others is tremendously fulfilling because it's a promise given to us by Christ Himself.

*The Lord Jesus himself said:*
*"It is more blessed to give than to receive."*
*(Acts 20:25)*

## The reaction makes all the difference

If we examine just the physical and intellectual act of giving, it shouldn't be all that exciting. Giving something away should not give us the same pleasure as getting something from someone. In reality, the flesh doesn't get too wound up when it's giving, but it certainly has a hard time sitting still when it's getting. Obviously the Lord knows this; so was He wrong to say, "It is more blessed to give than to receive"? That of course is a rhetorical question.

The reason Christ said what He said is because there is a great blessing we receive when we're giving to those who fully appreciate it. Joy is imparted to the giver when those we're giving to react in delight to our gift. The reaction of the receiver makes all the difference in the world. Receiving the gift of encouragement is no different. By refusing to gratefully receive a person's encouraging words, you're depriving the encourager the opportunity of watching his gift getting unwrapped. The most exciting part of gift-giving is experiencing the delight on the face of the receiver.

Speaking from personal experience, whenever I buy my wife something, I have the most difficult time waiting until our anniversary or her birthday to give it to her. Seeing the elation on her face the moment she unwraps it is something I have a hard time waiting for. I think most men are like that. I'm convinced that's the reason almost every guy waits until Christmas Eve to do his shopping. The anticipation is too much to take.

Women don't seem to share that same inclination; my mother, for example, has most of her Christmas shopping completed sometime before Labor Day. If we men bought our gifts that early, the tree would have to be going up around Halloween. This next statistic has never been verified but you'd have a hard time convincing me otherwise. Ninety-eight-point-seven percent of all men missed receiving the gene that compels humans to shop. On the other hand, one-hundred percent of women get it. I've not been told this, but I believe the shopping gene attaches itself to estrogen at conception. As a man who obviously missed the gene, I shop infrequently, and when I do it's for very brief periods of time. You could say it's really a toss up for me, going to the mall or having my hip replaced.

Now, because of my lack of zeal to shop and the infrequency with which I do, I must be both imaginative and spot-on when procuring gifts for my wife. Not to toot my own horn or anything, but it's uncanny how often I have left a department store, after less than fifteen minutes mind you, knowing in my heart (deluding myself) that I have just purchased the one gift Michele can't do without (never in a million years would she have even thought to buy this gift for herself). Upon giving such a matchless gift, we men now need to be reinforced (multiple times) that it truly is one of a kind, and our wives' reaction will inform us immediately she thinks so too.

I have to say, Michele is well aware of this intrinsic desire (irrational compulsion) I have to be reinforced, and she always reacts quite passionately to all my gifts. Plus, as sensitive as she is, she's been known to wait as long as three days before inquiring whether or not I've kept the receipt.

### Being thankful encourages the encourager

Turning away someone's encouragement or reacting less than favorably towards it not only deflates the encourager's enthusiasm, but also it discourages them from encouraging again. If you have had problems in the past of being a good encouragee, try thinking in terms of that encouragement being a gift all wrapped up with your name on it. React how you would if you'd just been given something from your favorite store. Tell them how much their words encouraged you; after all, that was their intent. At the very least, smile and say "thank you."

Oh, and don't feel compelled to immediately respond to their encouragement with encouragement of your own. It will probably sound as though you're reacting out of an obligation rather than out of appreciation. You'll get plenty of opportunities later on to share with them some sincere encouragement at an appropriate time. Just keep in mind, reacting enthusiastically to the encouragement of others has the power to complete the pass and encourage the encourager in the process.

### Remember...
- Encouragement takes the full cooperation of no less than two people, the encourager and the encouragee.
- You have to learn to become a good receiver. The full validation only comes after you successfully receive the encouragement thrown your way.
- Think of all encouragement as though it was a personal gift all wrapped up with your name on it.

### It's your turn to be Jerry Rice...
No less than two of the quarterbacks Jerry Rice received passes from are in the Pro Football Hall of Fame. It's a given they are Hall-of-Famers, due in large part to Jerry's ability to validate them. You can do the same for anyone who takes the time and effort to encourage you. Start right now. Show the next person who esteems you just how grateful you are for their encouragement by welcoming each word into your heart. Along with blessing your encourager, I can almost guarantee it will bless your *Head Coach* as well.

# 6

# If It Is Encouraging,
# Let Him Encourage

*We have different gifts, according to the grace given us.*
*If it is encouraging, let him encourage.*
*(Romans 12:6,8)*

The Bible tells us that the ability to encourage others is a gift from God. The Greek word used here for *encouraging* is translated as *exhorting*. Both words (encouraging and exhorting) carry the same meaning: "Words spoken to uplift another person."

Romans 12 is intended to inform the Body of Christ how we, as members of that Body, are to live daily. The apostle Paul begins the chapter by urging his readers to offer themselves as living sacrifices to God. In other words, we are to *give over* our will in an effort to have God's will become our desire.

Giving over our will to God is a difficult process. First, we have to wrestle it away from our flesh, and that is never easy. For many of us, living out the will of God is tremendously challenging because it means we have to get to a place where we are no longer in control. Now, if there's one desire all flesh has, it is to be in control.

When we begin debating with ourselves whether or not to give God the permission to manage our lives, the enemy, sensing he may be losing his grip on our flesh, will immediately use fear as a deterrent. Giving away control of anything becomes for most people a difficult process; and when that *anything* happens to be our lives, it's especially difficult. When we're no longer running things, we have to trust the one who is, and for the majority of people, that shift from trusting ourselves to trusting another can be fearful. The enemy knows all about fear; it's one of his most effective weapons, and he uses it liberally because he knows one of the last things any of us want to deal with is fear. God, however, saw that very thing coming and made provision for it.

> *There is no fear in love. But perfect love drives out fear,*
> *because fear has to do with punishment.*
> *(1 John 4:18)*

Giving our lives over to God is never fearful in application, only in thought. Once God has the reins, His perfect love takes over and we quickly realize His desire is only what's best for us. We also realize how foolish we were to have debated so long in giving Him those reins. You see, once God is in control, fear becomes a non-entity. Let's take a look at Paul's call for us to surrender our lives to God.

> *Therefore I urge you, brothers, in view of God's mercy,*
> *to offer your bodies as living sacrifices.*
> *(Romans 12:1)*

Paul was using the word *sacrifice* as a literal meaning, not as an analogy. He realized that a sacrifice doesn't get to determine its purpose. The purpose of the sacrifice is always determined by the One to whom the sacrifice is offered. As believers, we simply trust that God knows what's best and that He'll act in that knowledge.

In Romans 12, we learn that each one of us within the Body of Christ has been endowed with special gifts of grace. These gifts have a specific purpose: They are for the edification of the Body. In other words, every believer carries the potential for building and strengthening the members of Christ's Church. As its members become built up and made spiritually stronger, the Church itself reaps the benefits, and corporately the Body of Christ advances. The Church truly moves forward one believer at a time.

> *I tell you that in the same way there will be more rejoicing*
> *in heaven over one sinner who repents than over ninety-nine*
> *righteous persons who do not need to repent.*
> *(Luke 15:7)*

As those who have given themselves over as sacrifices, one extremely important responsibility we have within the Body is to exhort one another. By working to build each other up, we are doing our part in advancing the Kingdom. The problem has never been in possessing the ability to inspire and uplift our brothers and sisters in the Lord; the problem has always been allowing God to use us for this purpose. Too often the sacrifice wants to determine its purpose. It's my belief that everyone born of God has the ability to encourage others.

The Holy Spirit endows us with the characteristics of God, and one of God's greatest characteristics is that of encourager. Once we have received His Holy Spirit, we possess the power to live as Christ. As a matter of fact, we are expected to live as much like Christ as is humanly possible. No one has ever epitomized encouraging more than our Lord and Savior. Therefore, it should be a priority of ours to go about our day encouraging others as well.

**Encouragers need encouragement too**

While all children of God possess the ability to encourage others, I believe there are certain individuals who are given another *measure* of encouragement. That is the *charismata* (special gifts of grace) we find in Romans 12:6,8. This *charismata* is given to individuals as God subjectively determines. These are the people you know who seem to leave a trail of confident and inspired people everywhere they go. They are both passionate and non-discriminatory in their encouragement, and they hand it out as though they have discovered its eternal source. I find myself drawn to these people; after all, I have to honestly admit I *want* to be encouraged, I *desire* to be encouraged, I *need* to be encouraged!

Those with this gift of encouragement sense my need and my desire, and never fail to validate me; and the results are always the same. Remarkable! It's like receiving a spiritual shot in the arm. I always seem to walk away from these special people of encouragement with a renewed sense of strength. That's the true purpose behind it. Because with this renewed sense of strength, I can go out into the world more confident and more courageous, two qualities the world is not seeing enough of in the lives of Christ-followers.

Now, may I suggest something here? After being encouraged by one of these *messengers of God*, take a moment to bless them. Let them know just how much you appreciate what they do and how it truly makes you feel. Encouragers need to be encouraged too.

**Only God is capable of transforming lives**

The desire to encourage others may not be one of the special *gifts of grace* God has blessed you with. However, that doesn't preclude you from encouraging. As a child of God, your responsibility is to supply any need to anyone in need. It may not come as naturally to you as it does to others. It might even feel a little awkward when you speak encouragement to someone, but that's okay. All that means is you might have to rely upon the power of the Holy Spirit to carry it out for you, and I can speak from experience, that's never a bad thing. I mean, if all we did as Christians was to go around doing the things we were comfortable doing, how much of the character of God would others be introduced to?

When we're comfortable, we have a tendency to do things under our own power. By operating our lives under our own power, others only see and hear *us*, and while that by itself may not necessarily be a bad thing, that by itself will never transform lives. Only the power of God is capable of doing that. Christ dwells within us for many reasons, none of which is more important than enabling us to do things we can't do, or things we don't want to do on our own. When we begin doing that which God is calling us to do, we quickly realize we are not only out of our comfort zone, but also we are out of our ability zone. Encouraging and edifying others is a behavior most of us discover can only be done by the power of God.

When God supplies the power and you permit Him access to your mouth, two things will happen. Lives will be transformed, and God will get the glory. If you follow the life of Christ, you'll see those are the two things He was concerned about the most.

A couple of things Jesus never concerned Himself about were recognition and acclaim. He was too busy recognizing others and acclaiming his Father in Heaven. Recognizing others by encouraging them to continue this race called life is one of the most important responsibilities we have as the family of God. As God's children we are endowed with many of our Father's attributes, attributes that are given to us by the power of the Holy Spirit. We possess those attributes for a purpose; to give them away.

You read earlier in this chapter that one of God's special gifts of grace is encouraging. Now, encouraging is something that cannot be appreciated until it's given away. What good would it do us to have a special ability if we never put that ability to use? That's true of all of God's gifts. They are given to us for the express purpose of imparting them to others. Having the gift of encouraging is only beneficial if we spend our time handing out encouragement. I guess we could go around telling ourselves what an awesome person we are, but I'm pretty sure that's not what our gifts are intended for.

The gift of encouragement may not look as important as some of the more sought after gifts, but I'm convinced there isn't another gift God gives us that has more power to transform lives. Don't downplay the role encouragement has in helping to build others, as well as build up the Kingdom of God. And don't downplay your role as a purveyor of that encouragement. After all, the ability to encourage isn't something you've mustered up on your own. That ability, along with any ability that impacts lives and transforms people, can only come from God.

### Remember...

- Giving our lives over to God is never fearful in application, only in thought.
- The Holy Spirit endows us with the characteristics of God, and one of God's greatest characteristics is that of encourager.
- Having the gift of encouraging is only beneficial if we spend our time handing out encouragement.

### Don't wait for some kind of sign

The moment the Holy Spirit takes up residency in our bodies, we instantaneously possess the ability to demonstrate the character of Christ. Nothing epitomizes the character of Christ more than encouraging others. If you want to remind others of Jesus, simply give away God's gift of encouragement. But don't wait around thinking you need to *feel* something special first. You already are something special; you are a Spirit-filled child of the Living God! Just go about your day seizing opportunities to enhance the lives of others by speaking into them words of strength and exhortation.

**Part 2**

# Targets for Encouragement

*While our encouraging words should never be targeted exclusively to selective individuals, this section simply makes us aware of people we may be overlooking in the daily distribution of our inspiring words.*

## 7

# Encouraging Those
# Who Encourage Us

*By all this we are encouraged.*
*(2 Corinthians 7:13)*

For the past fifteen years, I have been greatly encouraged by a coworker who is the mother of an adult child with cerebral palsy. Cindy has cared for her son Jamie, primarily as a single parent, since his birth. She is an amazing mother who demonstrates on a daily basis the literal definition of unconditional love.

Having known a good number of such parents, I have found there to be common threads connecting every one of them. The first thread I find is the lack of resentment for having a child with a disability, even though no one would ever blame them if they did harbor a little bitterness. Another thread I find is their uncommon gratefulness for having this child in their life; it's as if they've chosen to view their child as a blessing rather than a burden. That perspective has to be through the enablement of God, because those of us looking from the outside in find it almost unimaginable placing ourselves in their shoes. And while we cannot envision the difficulties found in their situation, we can and often do, use their situation as inspiration to thank God and count our blessings that our lives possess no such challenges.

Their circumstances and how they have chosen to deal with them encourage the rest of us to keep going as we face problems of much less severity in our lives. Our motivation is, if they can do what they do every

59

day of their lives, then I can handle what I'm facing today. While we look to these remarkable people for inspiration and strength, we rarely if ever tell them how highly we respect them for their perseverance and their commitment. Have you ever wondered why that is?

When we admire them for being such an inspiration to us, why don't we tell them? I mean, if ever there were people who could use some encouraging words, it would have to be these parents. As difficult as it has been to raise three healthy children with a strong loving partner next to me, the thought of raising a child with special or multiple needs is almost unfathomable. As difficult as it's been to foster the maturation process of my three children, I have to admit I'm helped all the time by the encouraging things they say:

- "Thanks, Dad, for caring as much as you do."
- "Dad, you've always been there for me, and I love you for that."
- "I know you're just looking out for my best interest Dad, and I want you to know I appreciate you."

(Naturally as they were growing up we had to battle through the, "you're the worst dad ever" phase, which we did. Now that they are adults, they've become much more paternally astute.)

### Little arrows of encouragement

Those little arrows of encouragement our kids shoot our way from time to time go a long way in getting us over the hurdles we have to face. Parents of handicapped children don't always receive those arrows of encouragement, especially if their children are unable to express themselves verbally. I know they'll tell you they receive encouragement from their child in lots of other ways, and I'm convinced they do. I just know it's nice to hear the actual words of affirmation from time to time. So here's where we come in.

While many children are prevented from shooting verbal arrows of encouragement and admiration to their parents, due to their disability, those of us with knowledge of these families have no such limitations. And since these people provide us with the courage and the inspiration needed for us to continue on in life, we have an obligation to tell them. We can be supplying encouragement to those who supply it to us by letting them know how much we marvel at the way they live their lives. If these parents were to hear how much their living example means to us, it just might help encourage them to face their next tomorrow.

My daughter Jessica has, for the last six years, befriended Gabby, a nine -year-old girl with autism whom she began working with in a federally subsidized pre-school. Immediately there was an amazing connection. Jessica found herself being inspired and encouraged by this little girl and has spent a great deal of time with her outside of school. And while Gabby has made some great strides under Jessica's tutelage, she remains very dependent.

It's not uncommon for Jessica to babysit Gabby on a Saturday or Sunday, and most of the time it's at our house where our entire family has been able to fall in love with this little girl. Depending upon the day, her medication or a slew of other factors, as loving as Gabby is, the truth is, she can be a handful. What helps to make it bearable for Jessica when Gabby acts up is knowing she'll be going home in a few hours. The stress and tension Jessica experiences with Gabby is made tolerable by realizing she doesn't have to wake up and face those challenges every day. Gabby's parents aren't presented with that option; nor are the millions of other parents who love and care for their children with disabilities.

The following letter is intended as encouragement for all the loving, caring parents of children unable to voice their affection and appreciation for everything their parents have done and are doing for them. Just because their children aren't able to tell their mom and dad audibly how much they love them certainly doesn't mean they don't experience a deep and an adoring love for them. This letter is also intended to encourage parents of disabled children who provide for all of us a model of commitment, devotion and personal sacrifice.

*Dear Mom, Dear Dad,*

*First of all, let me start out by telling you how much I truly love you. And if there's anyone who can understand love, it's me, because I have the complete and exhaustive definition of love for a mother (father). You cannot possibly know the full extent of my feelings for you and what you mean to me.*

*From the time I was a baby until now, you have unconditionally cared for me with amazing commitment and faithfulness. You have sacrificed a huge part of your life to make mine so much better. Please don't think for one minute that I'm not aware of every little thing you've done for me, because there's not a thing you've done for me, I don't remember. Not one minute goes by that I don't thank God for having you as a mother (father). You feed me, you dress me, you bathe me, and through it all I have never once sensed anger or bitterness.*

*If I could, I would apologize for making you miss out on all the things other mothers (fathers) get to do with their children. Don't get me wrong, I wouldn't want you any other place but right next to me, because you see, that's when I'm the happiest. I'm never more content or more secure then when you are so close to me I can smell you. There's nothing that gives me more pleasure than your smell. Before I can hear you or feel you, your scent lets me know my mom (dad) is somewhere nearby, and it brings me immediate comfort. I can always tell you by your touch too, because it's always so soft and consoling. Nobody else's touch does that to me accept yours. God knew what He was doing when He compared gentleness with the way a mother cares for her child.*

> *But we were gentle among you, like a mother*
> *caring for her children.*
> *( 1 Thessalonians 2:7)*

*I think about what other children are capable of doing that I'm not, and I wonder sometimes what it would be like to do some of those things. However, if given the opportunity to do one thing, I know immediately what it would be; I would choose to put my arms around you and hug you all day long. I can't imagine anything feeling better than that! I know you get tired, Mom (Dad), and I can't help but feel responsible for that, but I want you to know that this is not all there is. I don't know how I know, but something inside me has promised there's a whole lot more after this life is over. I also know what's coming next is going to be way different.*

*So please, Mom (Dad), hang in there because what's coming next is indescribable, and I want to experience it all with you. I also know what comes next is going to make us forget all about this life; not that I want to forget about you or all that you've done for me, because nothing could be further from the truth. I'm thinking about you, Mom (Dad), and all the things you've had to do and to be, on account of me. Sometimes when I see the strain in your face or feel the tension in your body, I just want to cry out, but God is there to console me. He lets me know that something is coming way beyond our expectations and imaginations. He says that in the life that is eternal, there won't be any cerebral palsy, autism, or any other debilitating disease. As a matter of fact, He says there won't even be anymore crying or even pain. So you see, Mom (Dad), it is going to get better, a whole lot better!*

*All my love,*
*Your Child*

*Remember...*
- These remarkable parents who provide us with strength and inspiration for our lives need to hear how much we admire and respect them.
- If these parents were to hear how much their living example means to us, it just might encourage them enough to get through life's next trial.
- If someone has been for you a model of commitment, devotion, and personal sacrifice due to the unselfish way they live their life, find a way to tell them.

*Challenge yourself*

It's sad to think how often our admiration for someone's way of life never gets communicated. Given the opportunities we have every day to inspire and encourage those who encourage us, we are without excuse. Parents of disabled and handicapped children are such sources of inspiration to those of us who never have to shoulder that yoke in life; yet that inspiration, far too often, never reaches the ears of those who supply it. Why not sit down and make a list of the moms and dads you know who qualify as inspirational parents; just don't end it there. Challenge yourself to contact them personally and inform them of the encouraging role they have played in your life. Chances are your efforts will spring forth a blessing.

*Author's Note:* Since this chapter was written, Cindy's son Jamie became afflicted with pneumonia and within a few days passed away. Talking with Cindy, she voiced to me that she has no regrets and feels a sincere peace. It's easy to understand why. Her son has been set free from cerebral palsy, and just like in the above letter, it has gotten for him, a whole lot better!

# 8

# Encouraging Our Spouses

*Each one of you also must love his wife as he loves himself,*
*and the wife must respect her husband.*
*(Ephesians 5:33)*

I t's amazing; the very people we're closest to, those with whom we have chosen to share the rest of our lives, are usually the last ones to benefit from our encouragement. People to whom we have the greatest access are those we hesitate to validate most. Why do you suppose that is? Do we assume they already know we love them and are proud of them, so therefore there's no need to express it? If so, that's pretty weak. Do we feel as though we encourage them enough in other ways? Just as lame. No, there really aren't any valid excuses for not regularly speaking an encouraging word to the love of our life.

*"Why should I encourage her; she never encourages me!"* Now there's an attitude that explains why eight-year-olds aren't permitted to marry.

*"I would encourage him if he ever did anything worthy of encouraging."* Excuse me, but when the apostle Paul wrote verse five of the thirteenth chapter of First Corinthians, what part of "love keeps no record of wrongs" did you not understand?

It really doesn't matter what your situation is, there will be opportunities when you can honestly and unashamedly validate your spouse, probably on a daily basis. However, I'm willing to bet the vast majority of you have trouble recalling the last time you verbally praised them. It's amazing to think we have an easier time offering complete strangers words of encouragement than we do the person to whom we said "I do." Why is that?

While I don't have the answer to that question, I can tell you that the studying and research I've done for this book has made me realize I have spent a lot more time sharpening my skills of sarcasm on my wife than I have honing a proficiency in praising her. I look back now on those times and shake my head, remembering all the precious moments I could have lifted Michele up but chose instead to berate the woman I'm madly in love with. The woman, who should be on the receiving end of some of my very best exhortations, has more often found herself at the back end of my jokes. Boy, do I have lots to make up for.

Thank God I can still do something about it. And here's what I'm going to do. As of this moment, I am committing myself to say at least one encouraging word to my wife every day. I figure we spend on the average of five to six waking hours a day in the same house, so I have plenty of opportunities to let her know how proud I am of the fact that she's the mother of my children and the woman I would choose all over again to be my wife.

How about you? How have you been doing in the area of exhorting and validating your spouse? Do you find it difficult esteeming your wife (or husband) verbally? Have you fallen out of the practice of saying something to your spouse, whether you are a husband or a wife, such as "Honey, have I told you lately that you are more attractive to me today than the day we got married?"

Now if exhorting your spouse hasn't been as much a daily practice as it has been more like every leap-year, you might want to ease into it slowly. For example, husbands, we wouldn't want our wives getting suspicious of what we might be up to. The fact that after saying something to her such as the above quote may cause her to be somewhat skeptical is in itself a clue as to the infrequency of which she's encouraged.

Let me ask you a couple of questions: Why is it that sending your wife a dozen roses is less awkward than speaking into her a bouquet of encouragement? When did whispering sweet nothings in her ear become whispering nothing at all?

### No shortage of marriage counselors

Think about this: We have more marriage counselors today than at any other time in our history and yet the divorce rate has never been higher. I believe communication or lack thereof is responsible for the vast majority of marital difficulties. Yet something as easy as a daily dose of encouragement has the power to cure even the most troubled marriages. Instead we'd rather spend ninety dollars an hour asking a licensed stranger to work it out. Talk about illogical.

Now I'm not naïve enough to think that all marriages on the brink of divorce today can be mended by the couples merely going around saying nice things to each other. However, if more encouragement were spoken to one another, I do believe there would be fewer marriages on the brink in the first place. Men, your wife has a need to be validated from time to time. Not only does she have a need, but she also has a *right* to be validated. That right belongs to her by the word of God.

> *Husbands, love your wives, just as Christ loved*
> *the church and gave himself up for her.*
> *(Ephesians 5:25)*

Loving your wife doesn't end with providing for her physical needs. Loving your wife incorporates everything needed to enhance her life, and that includes speaking words of encouragement. Sometimes encouragement is the only thing missing from an otherwise healthy and successful marriage. At the very least, how can speaking words that esteem your wife ever hurt? Put away your pride, men, and start taking the steps of strengthening your relationship via encouragement. The wonderful thing I discovered is the more you validate her the less you criticize her. And the more your validation becomes a frequent practice, the more you begin to see your wife as that woman worthy of the praise you're speaking into her. Not only that, but the more you esteem her, the more she portrays the woman she hears you esteeming. Always keep in mind:

> *A word aptly spoken is like apples of gold in settings of silver.*
> *(Proverbs 25:11)*

I'm willing to bet that all wives, even those who fancy nice jewelry, will appreciate even more your words of gold and silver than she will the real thing.

### The one thing husbands need

Ladies, Scripture commands you to *respect* your husband. To quote Mr. Webster, *respect* is "the quality or state of being esteemed." Thanks, Mr. Webster. I couldn't have said it better myself! Esteeming someone or something is to place upon them a high value. Let me ask, do you value your husband highly? Most women, when asked that question, are quick to answer, "Sure I do." Okay then, now how often do you tell him how much you value him? Would your answer be something like: "Hmm, let's see, there was that one time last summer when I came real close to saying something encouraging. Oh, wait, I know, when he fixed the furnace last Christmas, I distinctly remember telling him, 'I don't know what I'd do without you.'"

Not exactly the answer I was looking for. Ladies, let's say you were searching for the one thing to give your husband that would elevate his confidence and allow him to feel appreciated; what would it be? Okay, quit searching; I can tell you in two words what that would be: your endorsement. Nothing will validate him more than to hear his wife sincerely affirm him. When our wives affirm us, it carries with it a whole lot more weight than when someone else affirms us. You know why? It's because our wives know every one of our flaws, our imperfections; and when they choose to speak encouragement to us rather than something critical, our self-esteem skyrockets. We are, for the most part, insecure guys looking for approval, and when our wives provide it, we stop looking everywhere else for it. Perhaps Proverbs 22:1 says it best:

*To be esteemed is better than silver or gold.*

God has a word for everything, doesn't He?

Husbands handing out sarcasm and wives trying to recall the last time they esteemed their husband. This is not at all what the Lord had in mind when He created the institution of marriage. Husbands and wives are supposed to be one another's best friend; and what do best friends do? They support one another; they sustain one another; they affirm one another.

When we husbands look for occasions to validate our wives and you wives take advantage of opportunities to esteem your husbands, a healthy bonding takes place, and amazing things start happening in our marriages. By encouraging one another, little time is left for the enemy to get in and divide our relationships. Men, don't let another day pass where you fail to speak some word of encouragement to your wife. A little bit of advice here; don't wait until after she has just made your favorite meal either. Esteeming her for no other reason than because she is your wife will prove to be one of the most sensitive things you can ever do. Plus, it just might get her to prepare that favorite meal a little more often, even though that was not your motivation.

Women, hone your encouraging skills by speaking words of valida-tion to your husband. It's a great place to start; besides it will do wonders for his self-esteem. It's also something he truly desires. If you want to improve the relationship you have with your husband, all you have to do is begin to value him and his role as the husband with your words of affir-mation. Working together as husband and wife by validating each other just might lead to some awesome things taking place. If you want to know more about what those awesome things might be, I suggest you and your spouse begin reading together Solomon's Song of Songs. But before you do, you'd better check to see if the kids are asleep!

### Remember...
- Husbands and wives should be one another's best friend; and as best friends, we are to support one another, sustain one another, and affirm one another.
- Our spouses have a right to be validated.
- A daily dose of encouragement has the power to help cure even the most troubled marriages.

### Okay spouses, do your thing
Opportunities abound every day to validate and encourage our spouses. Too often we let those opportunities get away from us for no justifiable reason. That should not be. God has created the institution of marriage to bind husband and wife together as one. Nothing binds us more tightly than communicating how pleased we are with each other. We have no excuse for not speaking into our spouses words that build up their spirits and bestow self-confidence. If you are waiting for your spouse to change, consider this: The more you esteem your husband or your wife, the more they will begin to portray the person they hear you esteeming.

# 9

# Gossiping Encouragement

*Let your conversation be always full of grace,*
*seasoned with salt.*
*(Colossians 4:6)*

You're probably wondering why the title of this chapter combines two words that are diametrically opposite of one another: gossiping and encouragement. If you're like most people, you tend to see gossiping as the spreading of personal information about someone, usually of a negative nature, while encouragement you see as positive words spoken to esteem another person. If that's an accurate account of your definition, you'd be correct. Gossiping and encouragement, when placed together like this, exemplifies the term *oxymoron* about as accurately as any two words. If we look objectively at these two actions, given what we've come to know about gossiping and encouragement, we can pretty much agree that one is good and one is not so good. Scripture supports that statement:

*A <u>gossip</u> betrays a confidence.*
*(Proverbs 11:13)*

*Therefore encourage one another and build each other up,*
*just as in fact you are doing.*
*(1 Thessalonians 5:11)*

I don't think anyone has to read God's Word to tell them that gossiping is harmful and encouraging is beneficial. The vast majority of us have discovered, through personal experience, the pain caused by gossip as well as the pleasure received from encouragement. So knowing first-hand the pain gossiping can cause and knowing the good encouragement can achieve, why would anyone ever choose to gossip instead of encourage?

"Let's see, I can choose to denigrate a child of God, thereby reducing his self-esteem significantly, or I can choose to extol that same person and greatly enhance his level of self-esteem. Wow, tough choice. Rip someone apart or build someone up. Hmmm…let's see here…I'm sorry but I'm going to need more time." Ridiculous, isn't it? To even think we would take the time to mull that decision over in our minds is hard to imagine; yet we choose to gossip almost five-to-one over encouraging. Does that mean we're horrible people who have no sense of morality? No, what it means is that we choose to do that which pleases our flesh more often than we choose to do that which pleases the Spirit. Putting it another way; we do what comes naturally. We were born in flesh and we've been carrying it around with us since day one. Flesh is of this world, which makes it temporary and prone to sin. There's one thing all flesh wants to do. It wants to feel good. We can say our flesh is narcissistic. Since our flesh is prone to sin and is bent on feeling good, it will go out of its way to satisfy that desire. When we allow our flesh to get its way and satisfy its desire, it's a pretty good bet we're sinning.

**Gossiping is sin**

Gossiping is one of the strongest desires of our flesh; you could say our flesh *loves* to gossip. Think about it. When was the last time you turned down a juicy story someone offered to tell you about someone else? Gossiping is also sinning. It's considered a sin because of the destructive power it carries to crush the spirit of a child of God. We're not called to crush one another's spirit. Rather we're called to esteem each other's spirit:

> *But encourage one another daily, as long as it is called today.*
> *(Hebrews 3:13)*

One of the more unfortunate things concerning gossip is how we promote it. Every time we participate, either through listening or by personally speaking it, we are supporting and encouraging its harmful effects. Now for whatever reason, we tend to view gossip as one of the more "trivial" sins. (God's Word never categorizes sin; every sin regardless of our perceived magnitude causes separation from the Father.) Rarely, if ever, do we stop to think of the potential gossip has for destroying reputations, producing anxiety and depression for others, and damaging relationships.

*A gossip separates close friends.*
*(Proverbs 16:28)*

Gossips usually see what they're doing as harmless fun at someone else's expense. And if ever called to task on it, their reaction is likely to be defensive. "Come on, Reid, it's not as though I'm out there robbing and pillaging the community, for crying out loud. I mean there are a whole lot of other things way worse." I'm not so sure Jesus would agree.

*Let your light shine before men, that they may see your good*
*deeds and praise your Father in heaven.*
*(Matthew 5:16)*

I have a hard time believing that any form of gossip is synonymous with shining the light of God. Who would ever think to praise your Father in heaven after hearing you verbally abuse one of His children?

**Watch for things that satisfy our flesh**
When we hold such an innocent attitude toward gossiping, we're actually lending our support to what is being said. By merely listening to a person's disparaging words targeted at someone else, we're actually encouraging the gossip to continue spewing forth his or her verbal assault. How could that ever be considered even the least bit Christlike?

*With the tongue we praise the Lord and Father, and with it we*
*curse men, who have been made in God's likeness. Out of the*
*same mouth come praise and cursing.*
*My brothers this should not be.*
*(James 3:9-10)*

In the church we've learned to "preface" our gossip in an attempt to absolve ourselves from any guilt. Something like this, "Now you know I love her dearly and care deeply for her, but can you believe she would go and do something like that?" When we preclude our gossip with the "L-word," the only thing we're doing is compounding our gossip with a lie. For if we truly love the person about whom we are gossiping, we wouldn't be gossiping about them in the first place.

> *Love ...always protects.*
> *( 1 Corinthians 13:6-7)*

There's no such thing as innocent gossip and no such thing as innocent participation when it comes to gossip. To make matters worse, our guilt as "listeners" compounds the moment we run off and locate an accomplice willing to lend an ear to our verbal assault. And believe me, there's no shortage of those willing to lend an ear. That goes for those inside as well as those outside the church. It's incredible just how far people will go in an effort to participate in gossip.

In all honesty, gossip is unbelievably easy to find. If you're not hearing it at the water cooler at work or in the cafeteria at school, you can locate it anywhere on the internet or television. Cable TV is inundated with shows digging up anything they can to portray people in a negative light. And if they can't find something of substance, no problem, they'll just make something up. Next time you're waiting in line at the grocery store, read some of the headlines of the dozens of tabloids the store manager has so strategically displayed for you. Those (rag)azines carry some of the most outrageous and defaming accusations that could possibly be made about someone. The best thing you can do is save your money and refuse to support the vilification of other people.

As children of God, we should constantly be on the lookout for actions that satisfy our flesh at someone else's expense, and avoid them like the plague. Gossip is one such action. It has the potential of destroying so many lives because of the harmless attitude we've adopted toward it. Not only has God called us to avoid sinful and destructive action such as gossip, we are to go one step further and pursue the things of the Spirit.

> *So I say live by the Spirit, and you will not gratify the desires*
> *of the sinful nature (flesh). For the sinful nature desires what is*
> *contrary to the Spirit, and the Spirit what is contrary to the sinful*
> *nature. They are in conflict with one another so you do not do*
> *what you want.*
> *(Galatians 5:16-17)*

Avoiding gossip is not easy, as those who have attempted to do so can attest. As a matter-of-fact, it's one of the more difficult things we're called to do as children of God. One of the reasons it's so difficult is because of how inundated our lives are with it; even our lives within the church. That certainly should not be. Most of us are aware that Spirit-filled believers have no business participating in gossip. But because we're made of flesh, every chance the flesh gets to pursue its own desire, it will. While we're commanded not to participate, we find our spirit battling the flesh's craving to participate.

> *I do not understand what I do. For what I want to do I do not do,*
> *but what I hate; I do. For I have the desire to do what is good,*
> *but I cannot carry it out.*
> *When I want to do good, evil is right there with me...waging war*
> *against the law of my mind. (Romans 7:15,21,23)*

While this Scripture doesn't excuse us for choosing to sin, it does explain to us *why* we choose to sin. Gossip elicits an excitement within our flesh. The thought of hearing some exclusive information about someone else is stimulating, especially if it's not particularly flattering. By giving in to the urge to gossip, we are not living by the Spirit as we are commanded to do in Galatians; we're living by the sinful nature. We can't change the nature of our flesh, but we can change how we react to it.

## Encouraging others pleases the Spirit

When we "live by the Spirit," we search for the things that will please the Spirit; and when presented with the opportunity to please the Spirit, we choose to do so. Encouraging others pleases the Spirit. Every time the opportunity to encourage someone else presents itself and we follow through with it, we are living by the Spirit and accomplishing God's purpose for our lives at the same time. Just knowing *why* we sin has to help. We are not to let feelings determine our actions, but instead we are to base our actions on what Scripture, not our body, says. I'm going to throw out a question here that may get us thinking about gossip in somewhat different terms.

Why do we have to think negatively whenever we hear the word "gossip"?

I know Scripture portrays gossip in a negative light, but that's because whenever we read about it in Scripture, it pertains to the spreading of harmful information about someone else. Why can't we think of gossip in terms of spreading constructive information about someone? That's always bothered me about other words or phrases we've come to use only in negative connotations as well.

Take the term *peer pressure*. Those two words are always used in a negative light. We hear constantly, "Watch out for peer pressure; it could lead to abusing alcohol or drugs or some other form of delinquency." Why can't we put a positive spin on peer pressure and say, "Listen to your peers and follow their lead as they encourage you to make wholesome, moral decisions." It seems as though we've become a completely glass-half-empty society. Let's buck that trend and try encouraging others by gossiping. Not gossip as in spreading negative reports about someone else, but gossip as in spreading words that affirm someone else. Something like this:

"Did you hear what Kayla did? I heard she was at this party and some guys snuck in a bunch of alcohol. She told her boyfriend to take her home but he wanted to stay, so she called her dad, and he came and picked her up. Can you believe that? That girl has a lot more guts than I do!"

Contrary to what we've thought in the past, encouraging doesn't always have to be directed at the person being esteemed. Let others see and hear how you encourage someone who's not even around. Chances are, sooner or later, just like negative gossip, it will get back to them. But whether it gets back to the person being affirmed or not really isn't the important thing. The important thing is that what comes out of our mouth is now wholesome and glorifying to the Lord.

*Do not let any unwholesome talk come out of your mouths, but what only is helpful for building others up according to their needs, that it may benefit those who listen.*
*(Ephesians 4:29)*

Whenever we choose to (negatively) gossip, we're pretty much disobeying everything in Ephesians 4:29. We're letting unwholesome talk come out of our mouths; nothing is building anyone up; and we certainly aren't benefiting those who are listening. But every time we choose to build others up through gossip that is encouraging we are also speaking forth wholesome talk that will benefit those who listen, thereby obeying the Word of God.

I've got an idea; let's start a whole new trend of honoring people behind their backs. Be the first one in your circle of friends to validate someone when they're not around. Now that would be a pretty neat thing, wouldn't it? I wonder what would happen if people started going around spreading virtuous information about one another without some ulterior motive or expectation in return? I'm not sure, but I believe it has the potential to help transform lives.

*And we who...reflect the Lord's glory are being*
*transformed into his likeness.*
*(2 Corinthians 3:18)*

I can't think of anything that reflects the Lord's glory more than going around scattering righteous rumors about His children.

### Remember...
- Whether speaking gossip or merely listening to it makes you an active participant.
- Gossiping is a sin because of the destructive power it carries to crush the spirit of a child of God.
- Let's buck the trend of gossiping harmful information about others and instead esteem them by gossiping encouragement.

### It's a choice
Every time we participate in gossip, we do so by choice. While the urge to speak or hear gossip is one that is quite strong, we who take part in it are without excuse. God has given us all we need to overcome the temptation to gossip; He has given us His Holy Spirit. One of the functions of the Holy Spirit is to enable the believer to live self-disciplined (2 Timothy 1:7). Refusing to speak or listen to gossip will not be easy; every time it presents itself the opportunity, it becomes for us a choice. Something that will enable us to spread information about others and at the same time glorify God is gossiping encouragement. Choose to demonstrate the value you hold for another person's life by spreading positive and uplifting rumors about them. Just think how encouraged they would be to hear there are people out there telling others how much they admire and respect them.

# 10

# Headband Encouragement

*Do nothing out of selfish ambition or vain conceit, but in
humility consider others better than yourself.
(Philippians 2:3)*

A number of years ago when I was active in student council, I was
asked to head up a workshop for various local high schools in an
effort to bring those in leadership together and equip them with the tools
to successfully lead their student bodies. There were no less than a dozen
or so different seminars going on throughout the day from which students
could choose to attend. Each one had a different theme led by either a
guidance counselor or a student council advisor. All of them were benefi-
cial for helping build leaders, however, there was one seminar I attended
that day that made a lasting impression on me. I can't remember who the
facilitator was, but I certainly remember the impact she left on those who
were there.

The first thing the facilitator did was ask for six volunteers. She then
sat them at a table in the middle of the room and told them they were a
high school committee whose function it was to plan their homecoming
dance. There was no preset agenda; she merely gave them an assignment
and observed the interaction. After about five minutes or so, she stopped
the group. The next thing she did was to take out six headbands from her
briefcase and based upon five minutes of observation coupled with her
experience from doing this dozens of times, she carefully chose to match
specific headbands with specific students. Each headband had something
written on it that couldn't be seen by the person wearing it. The other five

committee members could read each other's, but not their own. The facilitator then told the committee to continue with their homecoming plans, only now they were to treat one another based exactly on what their headbands read; no exceptions.

To my recollection, the headbands read:

- *I am a natural leader*,
- *My ideas are always stupid*,
- *Ignore everything I say*,
- *Value my ideas*,
- *Laugh at my suggestions*, and
- *Compliment me*.

Immediately I saw her psychology in assigning the different headbands. To the one girl who barely spoke for the first five minutes, she tied on, *I am a natural leader*. To the boy who seemed to dominate the conversation, she assigned, *Ignore everything I say*, and so on. Wow, what an eye opener! Every time they needed something assigned or a direction in which to go, the entire group turned to the newly appointed *natural leader* for guidance. At first the girl was a little taken aback, but by the end of the exercise, she was like a completely different person. She was more expressive; she spoke with a great deal more confidence; and she even seemed a little disappointed when the exercise was over. On the other hand, the young man who everyone ignored became so frustrated that he had moved his chair away from the table by the middle of the meeting. The most intriguing part came as the group shared their feelings with the rest of us. Although they knew this was only an exercise, their headbands still had an amazing effect on their demeanor.

**What others say can affect our attitude**

What was written on their headbands didn't dictate their demeanor; it was how the others in the group treated them that did. The young man who wore the *Compliment me* headband shared how he heard more encouraging things said to him in that fifteen minutes than he had his whole life. The girl who wore the *My ideas are always stupid* headband shared how after her first two or three suggestions, she just gave up. She said she'd rather say nothing than get put down. At the very least, this short but powerful exercise demonstrates how the encouragement or discouragement of others can affect our attitude.

This proves to me, if someone could become validated and encouraged after role playing, what could they become after a daily dose of encouragement out in the real world? It excites me just thinking about it. Six people sitting around a table following the directions of a counselor they didn't know, and yet three of those people walked away from that table feeling much more esteemed than they had when they walked in. All of them knew it was an exercise, however, just hearing words of validation (never mind the fact they were manufactured words) made a positive impact.

That lesson really opened my eyes to the power our words can have on the lives of other people. There is something else to bear in mind here; while three people walked away from that teachable moment feeling pretty confident about themselves, there were three others who walked away emotionally wounded. Sure, it was only an exercise, but judging from the responses of those three, exercise or not, it hurt. I remember that the three people who were on the receiving end of the positive responses even apologized to the others when it was over.

### Every person has value

Maybe this would be a good time for you to examine your own life by asking yourself the following questions: Are there certain people in my life I have a tendency to ignore by devaluing the things they say rather than seeing the worth their opinions might hold? Are there others I rarely, if ever, compliment or esteem?

If you get real honest here, I bet you'll find there are some people you treat with a lot less significance than you do others. The truth is we all know better. Every person has value. And while we all can name one or two people who seldom seem to say much we consider worthwhile, there's one thing we should always consider: Their *lives* are very much worthwhile. That's what it truly boils down to. They are people, God's creation.

Through the experiences I've learned in this life, I've come to believe most people will live up to or *down to* the significance others hold of them. In other words, treat someone with contempt often enough, and chances are they'll become a contemptible person. By the same token, treat someone with value and significance, and chances are they'll become a person befitting of that value. It really comes down to treating people the way you want to be treated. Most of us learned this in Sunday school, but its wisdom carries through to us maybe even more as adults.

*Do to others what you would have them do to you.*
*(Matthew 7:12)*

Jesus had good reason for speaking this to His disciples; it was the same good reason Matthew had for writing it down. It's the truth. If we would all just live our lives following this simple philosophy, there would be no need for writing books explaining the benefits of encouraging others. Encouraging others would be something we'd just naturally do because of how much we enjoy hearing it ourselves.

There is so much merit in treating people with respect. That merit is discovered as we begin to place a value on life, every life, not just those we judge to be wise or knowledgeable. Every person has the potential to contribute positively to society, but too often they're not given the chance because for some reason or another someone has labeled them with a head-band that reads *My ideas are always stupid* or *I'm not as good as other people.* I'm awfully glad I'm not judged by some of the stupid things that come out of my mouth. Thank you, Lord. As for being good, well, let's just say Paul addressed that in the third chapter of his letter to the Romans when he said:

> *There is no one righteous, not even one; there is no one who*
> *understands, no one who seeks God. All have turned away, they*
> *have together become worthless; there is no one who does good,*
> *not even one.*
> *(Romans 3:10-12)*

The goodness and the righteousness Paul writes about here speaks to the self-appointed goodness and righteousness we desire to apply to ourselves. We look at other people and almost immediately begin to sub-jectively award ourselves with the *I'm better than they are* distinction. Paul explains that all of us have a sin problem, and all the self-attained goodness and righteousness we apply to our lives will never be good or righteous enough to earn the grace and mercy of God. That can only be attained by receiving the goodness and righteousness of Jesus.

> *But now a righteousness from God, apart from law has been*
> *made known...this righteousness from God comes through faith*
> *in Jesus Christ to all who believe.*
> *(Romans 3:21-22)*

So you see, every one of us are, in reality, wearing headbands reading:
"Not moral enough on my own"
"Can never be good enough"

"Worthless in accomplishing eternal things"

But the beauty of God is the person each of us becomes through His grace. So that once that grace is received, everyone can walk around with headbands reading:

"My Father calls me His own"

"He has made me righteous"

"I am blameless in His sight"

When we understand there is but one way to attain eternal goodness, we're not so apt to label others in a negative light. And when we come to realize we're all in this together, we will begin to see others, not for who they are but for who they were created to be, precious and priceless in their heavenly Father's eyes. This in turn should cause us to choose the words we say to one another very carefully. I mean, why would we berate someone our heavenly Father deems as precious?

If nothing else, I hope this chapter has made you aware of the authority each one of us holds in our words and our attitudes that can either unleash the potential in others or work to destroy that same potential. The amazing thing is that the key is in our hand. It truly boggles my mind to think that by choosing certain words to speak into another human being, I can either build them up or I can tear them down. What incredible potential the spoken word carries. I'm willing to bet, if we were to make visible our desires, each of us would be wearing invisible headbands every day that read:

"Please validate and encourage me"

I have an idea I would love for you to try. Next time you run into someone you tend to ignore or somebody you've criticized in the past, just pretend they're wearing one of the headbands from the seminar exercise. Visualize something of value, something that will cause you to speak words of affirmation to them. Even if what they have to say isn't the most profound thing you heard that day, so what? You're esteeming them as people not as philosophers. My guess is, not only will they walk away from your conversation feeling better about who they are, but so will you!

*He who refreshes others will himself be refreshed.*
*(Proverbs 11:25)*

### Remember...

- Don't ever underestimate the amount of power the spoken word has on influencing the attitude of other people.

- If you don't have something nice to say about someone...find something. Ignoring people will adversely affect their self-esteem as much as criticizing them.
- Make the effort to see the potential for goodness in other people.

### Put others in your place

This is just a little twist on the saying "Put yourself in the other person's place." The thought process is, in doing this, we'll better understand why others are the way they are, which will in turn allow us to develop more patience and become less judgmental. But if we *put others in our place*, not only will it cause us to be more patient and less judgmental, it will also enable us to treat them how we want to be treated.

> *Do not think of yourself more highly than you ought,*
> *but rather think of yourself with sober judgment.*
> *(Romans 12:3)*

# 11

# Self-Encouragement

*For the Lord will be your confidence.*
*(Proverbs 3:26)*

It seems as though we're always the first ones to question our own abilities. There's little to debate that we are, by far, our own worst critic. We tend to underestimate our capabilities and talents much too often while we tend to overestimate the competence and abilities of those around us. There's a simple explanation behind that practice. It's due to the combination of knowing ourselves too well and subconsciously keeping score, two actions that form a deadly arrangement.

You see, we have insider knowledge of not only every time we've messed up, but also we are made privy to the frequency of which we've messed up. That same information is not made available to us regarding everybody else. Since many of our mistakes seem to leave more of an impression on us than our successes, it's not long before we convince ourselves that our mistakes outnumber our successes five to one. Although we might not literally be keeping track of all our blunders with tally marks, we can easily become convinced they are probably somewhere in the bazillions. For far too many of us, we allow the knowledge of our failings to shake our confidence and bring about self-doubt. When we do that, no longer are we making decisions forged in self-assurance; instead we limp around in insecurity, questioning our next turn.

Keeping a subconscious total of all our mistakes is itself a big mistake. We don't do it for others nearly as critically as we do it for ourselves. Oh, sure, we're aware of mistakes others make, but since we have firsthand knowledge of every mistake we've ever made, we're under the impression that if our mistakes were bound and labeled, they would resemble a small reference section of the public library. It's amazing how critical we can be of ourselves. The truth is, everyone would have their own reference section of blunders. While it may be difficult not to critique the poor and inaccurate choices we've made in our lives, we should never throw those past performances back up in our own faces.

> *Love...keeps no record of wrongs.*
> *(1 Corinthians 13:4-5)*

How often have you read the above Scripture verse and applied it to yourself? I'm willing to bet...almost never. God is describing unconditional love here. He's telling us what it is to love *agape* style. Believe it or not, this verse was written for us to apply to our own lives just as much as it was written for us to apply it to the lives of others. It's virtually impossible for us to go around loving other people if we can't love ourselves.

**We have to be willing to forgive ourselves**

A surprising revelation came to me once I began offering counseling services. I discovered there are a whole slew of people out there who have difficulty liking themselves, let alone loving themselves. If there were a way to make public the number of people who struggle to love themselves, I believe that number would astound most of us. This may be met with some raised eyebrows, but I can say with strong conviction that a lot of people have an easier time looking past the misdeeds of others than they do looking past their own.

While that may not be true for everyone, I'm convinced there are far too many believers going around weighed down unnecessarily by past failings. I also believe their proclivity to carry that unnecessary weight has everything to do with their view of grace. They see their past as being so unworthy that they've turned God's grace into something they need to earn. The more we come to know the Scriptures, the more we see them guiding us as to how we're to treat others.

> *In humility consider others better than yourselves.*
> *(Philippians 2:3)*

It's a biblical progression from there to begin applying grace to other people, but for some reason we hesitate to apply it to ourselves. I think one of the main reasons is the intimate knowledge we have of just how unde-serving we believe we are. Our personal collection of errors, offenses, and transgressions contribute to our hesitancy to receive fully the gift of grace. Even though we read in Scripture that it's our responsibility to afford grace to *all* offenders, somehow we don't see ourselves included in that *all*.

*Forgive as the Lord forgave you.*
*(Colossians 3:13)*

Just as you read a moment ago how we're not to keep a record of wrongs perpetrated by anyone (including ourselves), this Scripture from Colossians is also intended to be self-inclusive. Forgiveness must begin at home. We have to be willing to forgive ourselves, yet so many of us struggle to do so. Whenever we have a problem forgiving someone we know, we're able to go to Scripture or take our unforgiveness to the Father, and He gives us the ability and strength to carry it out. While that practice of going to the Father for other people will forever be a work in progress, we almost never go there when it comes to finding forgiveness for our-selves. Instead we attempt to bury our personal unforgiveness somewhere in our subconscious and move on; only we can't really move on because we're forever reminding ourselves of our inadequacies.

People are only able to move on in life after they've encountered grace. Grace is what gives us that fresh start every morning. Grace is that second, third, and fourth chance at getting it right. However, grace is also God's permission to not only forgive ourselves but also to shred our com-piled works of mistakes. Most of us are aware that God's grace is afforded to us; we just have a hard time applying it.

The first step to take in practicing self-encouragement is to afford our-selves the same grace we're giving to others. In other words, we have to quit being a record keeper of all our mistakes. Successful people aren't successful because they never mess up; successful people are successful because they have mastered the art of keeping no record of wrongs. Self-confidence far too often is based solely on previous success; and if our most recent success isn't very recent, that can influence our attitude the next time we have to make an important decision. When we experience a couple of bad choices and wrong decisions in a row, we can begin to distrust our capacity to make any right choices. And that can lead to the *what ifs*:

- *What if* I fail again?
- *What if* I'll never be able to do it?
- *What if* they don't pick me?
- *What if* I never get a job?
- *What if* something happens to my kids?
- *What if* I never get married?

We even start obsessing over what we see as *potential* inadequacies, and when we do that, panic mode is right around the corner. Immediately, fear begins to have its way, and once we give it permission to invade and permeate our lives, our entire foundation gets shaken and we become transformed into the Cowardly Lion from the *Wizard of Oz*, convinced we cannot possibly stand up and be the man or woman we were created to be. If nothing else, take comfort in knowing we've all been there at one time or another.

**Our greatest source is the Bible**

I've been coaching high school athletics for the past thirty-seven years. I find it amazing that regardless of how talented my softball teams are, regardless of what they accomplish on a regular basis, every time we line up to play another talented team or ranked opponent, I tend to find myself going through the *what ifs*:

- *What if* we can't hit her rise ball?
- *What if* we don't get our bunts down?
- *What if* we're too tight?
- *What if* we're too loose?

It's as though I'm playing a *high-light* reel of my opponent in my mind and at the same time watching a *low-light* reel of my team. I start to focus on all our negatives, and that causes me to view my team as less-than-worthy. I find myself thinking, "In order to win today, we're going to have to play the game of our lives." I'm inclined to give far too much credit to the opposition and far too little credit to my team. I've figured out why. It's because I know everything there is to know about my team. I'm with them every day. I see every mistake they make in practice; I know their every flaw, every weakness, and I tend to let those weaknesses overshadow all their strengths, which by the way are many.

I focus on the opposition exploiting all those weaknesses and begin to wonder whether or not we even belong on the same field. Thank goodness,

I eventually catch myself, and the moment I do, I begin recalling and visualizing all the great plays my players are capable of. I center my thinking on their potential and all the times in the past where they came through with flying colors. That line of thinking enables me to conclude that our team is here because we deserve to be.

By shifting my focus to our abilities and away from our inabilities, I quickly regain confidence and begin to see my team not only as worthy, but also I see my team as victorious. The thing to bear in mind here is that nothing changed other than my mind-set. My girls didn't all of a sudden become better players. I merely quit dwelling on the things that could go wrong and instead began encouraging myself by calling to mind all the things which in the past have gone right. Now, as the encourager and the motivator of my team, I'm able to convey an attitude of confidence to them as they run out on the field. That same philosophy holds true for every one of us.

Think personally, how often have you stopped yourself from attempting something because you thought there was a good chance of it not working out? Or maybe you convinced yourself because of previous failures, this next thing you were planning had no chance either. The proclivity to throw up past failings does nothing but keep the children of God from attaining greatness. And greatness is what our Father has created us to attain.

Keeping score of our defeats in life only serves to hold us back. That's not to say we aren't to learn from our past mistakes, because we certainly can. We're just not to let those mistakes paralyze us from ever walking out in faith once again. The devil claims a victory every time a child of God is kept from going back out onto the field of life with confidence and self-assurance following a defeat. His arsenal's greatest weapons are doubt and uncertainty. It's a natural inclination to question our own abilities from time to time; however, it's unnatural and unhealthy to go from questioning those abilities to obsessing over them.

The one thing that can prevent us from obsessing and seeing only the inadequacies of our lives is, of course, encouragement; and the greatest source of self-encouragement is the Bible. Next to being a book of love, the Bible is loaded with inspiring truth intended to increase our sense of worth. Within it we discover just who we are, God's children, holy and precious in His sight. Its words remind us over and over again where our ultimate strength lies. It speaks of an inner strength and confidence we don't have to try and muster up ourselves. It tells us that when our resources run dry, we can go to the ultimate source, Jesus Christ, and fill up on the living water that runs eternal. It reinforces to us continually that regardless of how many times we fall down, there is One who reaches out to us willing to restore us unto Himself.

> *Then Peter came to Jesus and asked, "Lord, how many*
> *times shall I forgive my brother when he sins against me?*
> *Up to seven times?" Jesus answered, "I tell you, not seven*
> *times, but seventy times seven."*
> *(Matthew 18:21-22)*

Jesus used the seventy times seven (490) figuratively. The arbitrary number was used to represent the infinite amount of times our Father has forgiven us and to demonstrate to us there are no number of set times that we're to forgive each other. Continually we're reminded we are created in the image of God, and therefore we are in possession of everything we need to succeed. The rewards of following a forgiving God are without limit. He promises that any mistake we make can be made right through the action of confession and repentance. We're told that the God we serve doesn't keep score. We are reminded of our access to a power source that is timeless and ceases not.

We read about saints of the past who came to the end of their rope, only to receive the strength to go on and ultimately rise above. By simply reading the *Truth* found in Scripture, we can rediscover not only our purpose in life, but also the authority needed to carry it out; and the moment we rediscover our purpose, it's like a whole new dose of courage has found its way into our lives. That's the power found only in the Word of God. We can read heartwarming and motivational stories found in inspirational writings such as *The Readers Digest,* and while those stories can temporarily encourage us, they can't *supply* us with the power of renovating our way of thinking. Only God's Word has the ability to do that.

> *Be transformed by the renewing of your mind.*
> *(Romans 12:2)*
>
> *Be made new in the attitude of your minds.*
> *(Ephesians 4:23)*

The reward of encouraging others is tremendously satisfying, as are the rewards associated with the self-encouragement found in our relationship with Christ. While this chapter is titled *Self-Encouragement,* it might be more accurate if we just add a couple of words, something like, "Self-

Encouragement Discovered Through the Promises of God." We can find lots of ways to temporarily lift our spirits, but it's only through the confidence we gain through the Lord that we become truly and permanently encouraged.

## *Remember...*
- Keeping a subconscious total of all our mistakes is itself a big mistake.
- It's virtually impossible for us to go around loving other people if we can't love ourselves.
- Successful people aren't successful because they never mess up; successful people are successful because they have mastered the art of keeping no record of wrongs.
- The greatest source of self-encouragement is the Bible.

### Encouraging me, myself and I
You undoubtedly have done it for others, now go out and do it for yourself. Apply God's Word concerning forgiveness and love to your own life. Read over His words that teach us how to forgive as He has forgiven and how to love as He loves us. Make it personal. Then the only thing left is for you to go out and practice it. Don't allow past failings to keep you from attaining success in the future. That's the beauty found in the loving grace of God; no matter what yesterday brought, God is going to bring tomorrow!

*For everything that was written in the past was written to teach us, so that through endurance and the encouragement of the Scriptures we might have hope.*
*(Romans 15:4)*

**Part 3**

# Reasons for Encouraging

*Although our reasons for encouraging others is pretty obvious, it doesn't hurt to be reminded that esteeming them is not just our responsibility, it's also our privilege.*

## 12

# Why the Need for an Encouraging Book

*Surely no one lays a hand on a broken man when*
*he cries for help in his distress.*
*(Job 30:24)*

The title of this chapter is very close to being a rhetorical question. It's almost like asking, "Why the need for air?" All you have to do is read the morning paper, watch the evening news or just go about your day with your eyes fully open to the silent cries of others, and you have your answer to this chapter title. But maybe the question shouldn't be, "Why the need for an encouraging book?" Rather it should be, "Why are we allowing so many people to live their lives in discouragement?" There's far too much evidence pointing to the need for encouragement for anyone to dismiss whether or not we could use a bit more. A telltale sign that there's not enough encouragement going around is for you to answer the following question truthfully:

Could **you** use a little more?

Personally, I get encouraged quite a bit. As a pastor, just experiencing worship with others, praying for others, and seeing God work in their lives is a wonderful measure of encouragement; but given the daily pressures of leading a church body, I have to tell you I could use a little more. Having an awesome marriage to a beautiful Christian woman for the past thirty years has been a tremendous source of encouragement; however, in the attempt to love my wife as Scripture tells me, I could stand to use a little more. The three healthy children God has blessed me with and a son-in-law who loves the Lord provide me with no small quantity of encouragement; yet in an effort to come alongside and assist them with the pressures they continually face, experiencing a little more encouragement wouldn't hurt. Being surrounded by co-workers who inspire me on a daily basis brings me a great deal of encouragement; but because of the societal demands on Christians in the marketplace, I am constantly looking around for a little more.

You may find me a bit greedy, desiring to hoard all this encouragement for myself and all, but the fact is, there's no such thing as being encouraged too much. You see, there is an endless supply of it out there, and the vast majority of it remains untapped. Plus, being encouraged restores me and enables me to feel good about myself; and let me tell you, I'm no different from anyone else when it comes to wanting to feel good. What I hope you realize is this: While I receive no small amount of encouragement from a good many sources, I still have a need and a desire to be further encouraged. And if I have a need, given the fact I'm being encouraged on a daily basis, just imagine all those who are getting little or no encouragement at all.

**Nothing more precious than children**

Having taught in the public schools for thirty-seven years, I have had access to thousands of lives. I can't begin to tell you how many of those lives are attempting to function in this world without any encouragement. I just told you how many sources of encouragement I have, and if I am to be completely honest, life can still be extremely challenging. I'm in no way attempting to say my life is full of hardships and suffering, because it's anything but that; however, if life can be difficult for someone such as myself from time to time, someone who gets validated a lot, how much encouragement is needed for those whose lives are full of hardships where validation is non-existent?

Children are looking every day for validation, and when they don't get it from their parents or their teachers, they go about trying to find it anywhere they can. Too often that means they resort to looking for it in inappropriate places. While the theme of this book is to emphasize positive and productive encouragement, be aware that the enemy uses encouragement too, only his encouragement leads to self-destruction. And let me say, where there's a void of valuable and constructive encouragement, there is no short supply of harmful and worthless encouragement going on. That's another reminder why this message of encouragement is so important. It's not enough that we battle the hardships and difficulties of this world; we are also fighting against a formidable opponent whose intention is to destroy anything God deems as precious. You don't have to be a theologian to realize that there's nothing God deems more precious than our children.

> *Let the little children come to me, and do not hinder them,*
> *for the kingdom of God belongs to such as these.*
> *(Mark 10:14)*

As a teacher, I see little ones "such as these" hurting for any number of reasons. Often those hurts are due to children being ignored or criticized by their peers. Some students are able to let hurtful things roll off their backs, while others take completely to heart everything they're told. I've counseled no small number of these students, and I find that those who have encouraging parents are a lot less likely to be seriously affected by the things their peers say. It's almost as if the encouragement given to them by their parents negates the malicious things others say. These children who are affirmed and blessed by Mom and Dad have a much greater chance of persevering through the testing times of life than those whose lives are void of such affirmation.

Children aren't the only ones battling discouragement and pessimism. Adults are just as susceptible, only in many cases, Mom and Dad aren't around to counteract the barrage of negative criticism they hear every day. Not everyone grew up in a home like I did where I was affirmed on a daily basis by my parents. I received the blessing from my father a long time ago and I no longer feel as though I have to go out and earn it from everyone else. It would astound you to know how many adults are still trying to earn their blessing, and when they aren't affirmed in everything they do, they retreat into a semi-depressive state, waiting for that next dose of validation to come their way. Far too often, it never gets there. It's my belief there would be a whole lot less Prozac being prescribed today if parents twenty years ago would have taken a moment every now and again to affirm and encourage their children.

### The good news is we can fix it ourselves

Why the need for this book? It's because while God has mandated His people to go out and speak encouragement into the lives of others, very few of His people seem to be willing to do so. Not having the experience of living through the Great Depression, I can't speak as to the general attitude of the nation at that time. However, I have a hard time believing the need for encouragement was any greater back then than it is today. While people may appear to be living at a higher standard in the twenty-first century, I question whether or not their actual lives are any less depressed. I can say rather confidently, I have yet to experience a time when the demand for people to be encouraged was so great and the supply of encouragers so low.

The good news is we can fix it ourselves. It's not something we have to wait for the government to do. We're hearing every day how horrible our health care system is. I have a solution. Instead of complaining about something we have so little control over, why not take the one thing we have complete control over, which is our ability to spread encouragement, and begin caring for the emotional health of others. There are millions out there in dire need of something we all have an infinite supply of.

Is it going to fix all our problems? Obviously not, but I can tell you this. By you making a concerted effort to encourage those around you, it will make a discernable difference in their lives; and from there only heaven knows what can happen as a result of the impact you've made. That's all any of us are called to do. Make an impact on the lives of others. God has given us the impact tools and He's given us unlimited opportunities. The rest is up to us.

> *You are the light of the world. A city on a hill cannot be hidden.*
> *Neither do people light a lamp and put it under a bowl. Instead*
> *they put it on a stand, and it gives light to everyone in the house.*
> *In the same way, let your light shine before men, that they may*
> *see your good deeds and praise your Father in heaven.*
> *(Matthew 5:14-16)*

The motivation behind this book is not an attempt to impart some great revelation; it is merely to remind us that as the children of God we hold the potential of greatly influencing the lives of others. That's an enormous responsibility. It's also an enormous privilege. By choosing to remain silent when we witness opportunities to speak God's encouragement, we are taking our lamp and putting it under a bowl. I don't know about you, but I'd much rather see God's light on a stand in the middle of the room esteeming everyone in the house.

Give it a shot; what do you have to lose? The worst that could happen is someone you know becomes encouraged; and after they do, they feel the urge to go out and encourage someone they know, and then that person goes out, and then that person goes out, and...well, you get the picture. But encouragement has to start somewhere. Let it start with you!

*Remember...*
- There are virtually millions of lives attempting to function in this world every day without the benefit of encouragement.
- It's an enormous responsibility as well as an enormous privilege to be able to positively influence the lives of others.
- It's not enough that we battle the hardships and difficulties of this world; we are also fighting against a formidable opponent whose intention is to destroy anything God deems as precious.

*We have to start somewhere*
In light of our call to encourage, it would be easy to get overwhelmed given the number of people living depressed and despondent lives. We could easily throw up our hands, shake our heads and say, "What's the use?" And while few would blame us, that's not what God expects from His people. One thing that might help is to take our eyes off the amount of work there is to be done and just focus our eyes on the difference we can make. That's all God is expecting. Make a difference right where you are. If it's a nursing home, a school, a corporation, a beauty salon, a department store, a prison, a truck stop, or your home, you have to start somewhere. And believe me, once you get started, don't be surprised when you find out just how difficult it is to stop.

# 13

# To Encourage:
# A Matter of Life and Death

Physiologically speaking, words may be just sounds formed by the shape of our lips and the positioning of our tongue as air is forced out of our mouth; but, in actuality, a great amount of significance is attached to each one. Far too often we dismiss the words we speak as unimportant and irrelevant. We attempt to trivialize our speech by saying, "What's the big deal, they're just words," but nothing could be further from the truth. Proverbs tells us of the potential power our words hold.

*The tongue has the power of life and death.*
*(Proverbs 18:21)*

There's nothing trivial about possessing that kind of power, and those in possession of that power must understand exactly what they are wielding. By using the term "life or death" to describe what our words are capable of, Solomon informs us of the potential we have for speaking either nourishment into the souls of others or toxin.

*The tongue of the wise brings healing.*
*(Proverbs 12:18)*

*A deceitful tongue crushes the spirit.*
*(Proverbs 15:4)*

Using his God-given wisdom, this King of Israel is letting the world know our words will have consequences; but rarely do we stop to consider the extent of those consequences. Every time we verbally communicate with another person our words are capable of impacting their lives in either a positive way or one that's not so positive.

I believe most of us are aware of the damage and pain hurtful words can cause. It's a good bet the majority of us have, at one time or another, been on both ends of cruel and offensive language. There have been books written, laws established, and workshops structured on the harmful effects of saying harmful things. My motivation for writing this book is to focus on the potential we all have of bringing life and restoration to our fellow human beings using positive words; words which will affirm and strengthen them. By using this power to validate those around us, we are executing God's desire for His children to speak blessings to one another.

*Do not repay evil for evil or insult for insult, but with*
*blessing, because to this you were called so that you may*
*inherit a blessing.*
*(1 Peter 3:9)*

Whenever we open our mouth and speak, it's by choice. Whatever words go forth from our lips they do so because we have chosen to release them. By choosing to release certain words, we option to support, energize, and empower those to whom those words are targeted. Those words are the basis of this book, they're called encouraging words. There are thousands of them. However, by choosing to speak words of a dissimilar nature, we have the option to sadden, depress, or dispirit those to whom we're speaking. Those words are called discouraging words; unfortunately there are plenty of those to choose from as well.

The choice of encouraging or discouraging is ours and ours alone. And as much as we want to blame others for things that we say, the onus falls completely on us. "He provoked me to say it" or "She said it to me first" are typical responses when we're confronted with something we've said that was particularly hurtful. We attempt to excuse our way out of responsibility because we know the moment that last discouraging syllable leaves our mouth, it should have never been spoken. That's why we should never say anything when we're angry. My goodness, we have enough trouble staying away from sarcasm and discouraging words when we're in a good mood. There is nothing good found in anger, and when we direct our words to someone we're angry at, there is zero chance of those words carrying with them anything even resembling encouragement. That's why the brother of Jesus wrote what he wrote.

> *Everyone should be quick to listen, slow to speak and slow*
> *to become angry, for man's anger does not bring about the*
> *righteous life that God desires.*
> *(James 1:19-20)*

When was the last time you spoke to someone out of anger and later determined it was the right thing to do? I would have to believe, if you're like the rest of us, the answer to that question is probably never. When we do speak out of anger, more often than not, we're sorry for it. Now there might be times when you were angry and it has caused you to speak up and say things you wouldn't normally say, and the result may have been positive. Maybe there was some injustice taking place, and you spoke up in a little louder voice than normal and got someone's attention that rectified the injustice. Those instances are very few and far between (unless you happen to be a school teacher!).

What is most common is to become angry at someone or at something someone did, and in that attitude of anger say something particularly hurtful, something you had to apologize for later, or should have. And while people appreciate it when we do apologize, our words of discouragement have already been received. The people we hurt in our anger might be willing to forgive us, but they don't have the option of forgetting what we said, ever. And ever is a long time.

We can attempt to excuse ourselves from the responsibility of the pain caused by something we said under the influence of anger by later confessing, "I didn't mean it; I was just mad," and while it may help some, it will never erase the words spoken. The one thing we must keep in mind is, regardless of what words we choose to speak, they are going forth with a great deal of power, power to heal or power to destroy. Unfortunately, it's not very often we take the time to consider the reality of that statement.

## The emotional equivalent to CPR

Just think how appalled you'd be to discover your doctor chose to give you the wrong medicine, not by accident, mind you, but that he weighed the options and decided to do so. Your doctor was given the opportunity to prescribe a medicine that would begin the process of healing and chose instead to give you a medicine that would make you more ill. What would your reaction be? I would think you would be appalled to say the least, and rightly so. "What were you thinking, doc! You had the perfect chance to make me well but chose instead to increase my illness?"

I personally don't know of any instance where a doctor chose to do that nor do I think any doctor ever would. However, I have known plenty of instances, many of them firsthand, where a small amount of encouragement could have gone out and quickly healed, but words of discouragement went out instead, and with them went destruction. What makes those instances even more disparaging is knowing they were carried out by choice.

> *With the tongue we praise our Lord and Father, and with it we*
> *curse men, who have been made in God's likeness. Out of the*
> *same mouth come praise and cursing.*
> *My brothers this should not be.*
> *(James 3:9-10)*

When we break it down like this, hurting people with our words is no less appalling than if our doctor opted to increase our sickness. Why is it we'll go out of our way to help someone in physical need and yet leave those in emotional or spiritual crisis unattended? Instances occur every day where we hear about people risking their lives to help perfect strangers. At the very least, when we see someone in need, our first instinct is to do whatever we can to alleviate his or her distress.

We're quick to call out, "Someone phone 9-1-1; this person needs help!" We'll even take a CPR class that by chance we run into someone in physical distress. Thank God most of us never have to put it into practice. Now, if we care this much about others that we'll take classes and learn techniques to save someone's life, why is it we refuse to come to the aid of someone suffering from an emotional affliction? Especially when encouraging someone doesn't call for us to run into a burning building, dive into a raging river or even call for an ambulance.

Encouragement can be the emotional or spiritual equivalent to cardiopulmonary-resuscitation, only it can be applied without any training whatsoever. What's more, it can be applied standing up, which makes it a bit more practical. Also, coming across a situation where CPR is called for would be nothing less than traumatic for the great majority of us; the stress alone would be overwhelming. On the other hand, applying encouragement to the heart of someone afflicted by discouragement would serve to alleviate stress in both them and us.

I have to believe those living with emotional scars and broken hearts are much more prevalent than those suffering cardiac-arrest, which gives every one of us ample opportunity to speak forth God's words of restoration. I'm willing to bet the vast majority of people we come in contact with every day are in need of some level of encouragement. And while there is no medical evidence to back this up, I question just how many heart attacks could be prevented by free-lance encouragers going forth speaking health into those in need.

One of the reasons I admire physicians so much is due to the amount of time they spend in training. Many doctors attend school for eight to ten years in an effort to obtain a license that will permit them to begin healing those who are physically hurting. It takes an incredible amount of work and commitment to become a doctor, and I'm told by a number of physician friends, the rewards of seeing patients healed and made whole again far outweigh the difficulties of getting through med school.

When you think about it, God has given each of us a license to go forth and apply the healing salve of encouragement to the hearts of all those suffering from emotional sickness. We have the same privilege a doctor has without all that studying and training. Every day we're provided the opportunities to restore and make whole people who are weighed down and encumbered by all kinds of emotional and spiritual maladies. The responsibility doctors have of healing others is so great that they have to take the Hippocratic Oath and pledge to "…prescribe regimens for the good of (their) patients according to (their) ability and (their) judgment and never do harm to anyone" (AMA website).

As children of God, we carry no less the responsibility of healing through the enablement of our Creator on an emotional level. Our oath is not taken from a fourth-century Greek physician, however; it is taken from the Word of God.

*Anyone, then, who knows the good he ought to do and*
*doesn't do it, sins.*
*(James 4:17)*

As you see, it's not enough for the children of God to merely abstain from doing sinful things and living sinful lives; our responsibilities to our brothers and sisters are much broader and run much deeper. We are expected to come to the aid of anyone we know to be in distress. And if we're truthful with ourselves, a day doesn't go by that we don't come in contact with at least one discouraged or distressed person. It's what we do with those opportunities we're presented with that will ultimately determine just how intent we are in living out our Father's command.

*Love each other as I have loved you.*
*(John 15:5)*

### Remember...
- The one thing we must keep in mind is, regardless of what words we choose to speak, they are going forth with a great deal of power.
- The vast majority of people we come in contact with every day are in need of some level of encouragement.
- By speaking forth encouragement, each of us has the potential of bringing life and restoration to our fellow human beings.

### Calling all physicians
Why not begin today practicing your skills as an emotional healer? Go forth and speak encouragement every chance you get. By doing so, you'll be personally writing the prescriptions and applying the medicine which will help restore those patients who would otherwise linger emotionally and spiritually wounded. In all reality, if we just live to carry out God's plan for our lives, there's no reason for anyone to live a wounded life; especially with the amount of medicine that's available. The only thing missing are the emotional doctors who are willing to write those prescriptions and take that medicine and begin directing it to the source of others' wounds.

*The harvest is plentiful but the workers are few.*
*(Matthew 9:37)*

If you read this Scripture verse in context, you will see Jesus calling all disciples to go about the towns and villages, preaching and healing. By making our daily rounds as spiritual physicians, we are adding to that much needed force of labor.

# 14

# Our Need to Be Encouraged

*In this world you will have trouble, but take heart!*
*I have overcome the world.*
*(John 16:33)*

In John 16:33, Jesus gives us the reality of two promises. First, He tells us our lives are destined to experience trouble in this world. I think every one of us can pretty much attest to that. If we go back a little earlier in the book of John, Jesus tells us why:

*If you belonged to the world, it would love you as its own. As it*
*is, you do not belong to the world, but I have chosen you out of*
*the world. That is why the world hates you.*
*(John 15:19)*

The phrase "the world" refers to the human system opposed to God's purposes. We know that system to be motivated by the prince of this world who is, of course, the devil. In Jesus' own words, He says, "The prince of this world stands condemned" (John 16:11).

It's a fact, we belong to either the Kingdom of God or we belong to the world. That fact is made evident in the Word of God.

*I tell you the truth, no one can see the kingdom*
*of God unless he is born again.*
*(John 3:3)*

By accepting the gift of God's grace and receiving the atoning sacrifice Jesus made for each one of us, we become children of God and, therefore, heirs to the kingdom. Regardless of our eternal citizenship, however, our temporary residence is this world. For those of us who are citizens of God's Kingdom, we learn rather quickly: That which opposes God opposes His people as well. In other words, we as believers have a common enemy, a relentless enemy, a ruthless enemy, an enemy who will stop at nothing to destroy our lives.

> *Be self-controlled and alert. Your enemy the devil prowls around*
> *like a roaring lion looking for someone to devour.*
> *(1 Peter 5:8)*

Peter didn't intend for this to be a simile; he intended it as reality. And since we have a common enemy, it only makes sense that we join forces in an effort to bring this enemy down. Our strategy should be cooperation and cohesiveness, a force of one if you will. Too often, however, we find ourselves attempting to battle this formidable opponent alone, and in so doing, we find ourselves black and blue, and plagued with weariness. Here is where we must trust in the second of Jesus' promises:

> *But take heart! I have overcome this world.*
> *(John 16:33)*

Jesus spoke these words for a specific purpose. He wants His children to realize that this world is capable of being overcome. Those of us who are *in* Christ *have* Christ. We have His promise and we have His power. That power which enabled Him to conquer the rulers, the authorities, the forces of evil in this dark world is available to every one of us. Jesus' promise to deliver His people into His Father's eternal Kingdom one day is our blessed hope, but to wait around for that day to appear as weary, worn and wounded soldiers is not what Jesus had in mind when He spoke this verse recorded in John 16. The truth of this verse could enable it to be interpreted as: "But take heart, I have overcome this world [for each one of you]." What we need to realize is, Jesus has provided for us a life here on earth that is much more than a way station to our next existence. Jesus' sacrifice covers this planet as well as our heavenly home. He wants us to experience the victory of overcoming the enemy right now!

*I have come that they may have life, and have it to the full.*
*(John 10:10)*

## God has given us each other for many reasons

It is our Lord's desire for us to live our lives in fullness. Fullness doesn't include anxiety, depression or fear. As a matter of fact, the word *full* as Jesus spoke it is translated in the Greek as *perissos*. *Perissos* is the antithesis of anxiety, depression and fear. It actually means "exceedingly abundantly above" or what sounds even better "superabundant"! Jesus came so that you and I, and all other believers, can live our lives as super-abundant people.

Now, I'm willing to bet the majority of us exist somewhere below the superabundant line. And one of the reasons we do has to do with how we're battling our common enemy, the devil. Too often we attempt to stand against him unarmed and single-handed. That's not wise. The enemy loves it when we come out to face him on our own; he has quite a reputation for winning when his enemy is both unarmed and unaccompanied. Knowing that, you'd think the last thing we'd want to do is face this adversary without any help, especially when all the help we need is but one encourager away. We have this common enemy, for crying out loud; doesn't it make sense for us to align together and go after him as a force of one? God has given us each other for many reasons; one of those reasons is so we can partner together and defeat this devil collectively.

One of the most effective ways of bringing the community of God together in an effort to defeat our hated enemy is to become an encourager. Encouraging is, in actuality, instilling confidence in the lives of others, a necessity when preparing for war. Merely by speaking words of life and health into one another, we are strengthening and energizing God's soldiers for the battles of life. When we choose to voice encouragement, we are assisting God in enabling His people to overcome this world. The mere thought of that should give us goose bumps. Imagine, little ole you and me assisting God! Exhilarating, isn't it? The best part is when we speak forth encouragement, it gives our lives great purpose, and pleases our heavenly Father as well. Those are two pretty lofty goals being realized through one simple action.

If each one of us would make a conscious effort to encourage one person every day, think of the impact we could have in helping others triumph over this world. Think of the impact others can have in helping *us* triumph over this world as well. The sooner we realize we're in this together and we begin collectively using the resources God has given us, the sooner we can experience the fullness of life God has promised.

## Our words affirm and give confidence

During times of war, commanding officers go to great lengths, as often as possible, to personally address their men in the field. Why? They do it in an attempt to fire them up and boost their morale, to encourage them. They understand a confident soldier is a more effective soldier. I'm sure you've seen war movies when the CO gets driven to the frontline, accompanied by his entourage amidst the soldiers' cheers, and delivers some highly inspirational message that invigorates the GIs to take the next hill or capture the next town.

And what would a good football movie be without some rousing half-time speech by the head coach? Lord knows, I've been a part of hundreds of locker-room talks throughout my coaching career, and every one of them had one intention: to encourage the players to go out there and defeat the enemy. I see nothing wrong with provoking a little adrenaline from time to time as a way of getting people to perform more effectively.

Now if encouragement works on the battlefield and it works on a football field, there is no reason to believe it's not going to work in the everyday trenches of life. The only thing about making this work in life is that each one of us will have to assume the role of commanding officer or head coach. It is the responsibility of each one of us to address the participants of life with words that inspire and motivate them. We know all too well that maybe the first half of life hasn't been too kind to some people we care about. It may be a result of something they've done or something beyond their control; it really doesn't matter. What does matter is that you and I must assume the role of head coach and speak into them words that affirm and give them confidence. They need to hear that the next hill or the next obstacle in their life can be overcome.

The best, most effective way to do that is through encouragement. The exact way you can encourage them is up to you and God; it's always a good thing to include Him in these kinds of things. As the Head Coach of the team and the Commanding Officer of the unit, He has the best handle on what to say and when to say it. He just needs a willing vessel to go forth and become His mouthpiece. Make it a practice to go to Him often and seek His counsel. He will give you exactly what needs to be said in an effort to help others overcome the challenges of life.

*Remember...*

- Since we have a common enemy, our strategy in battling this enemy should be cooperation and cohesiveness, a force of one, if you will.
- We need to realize Jesus has provided for us a life here that is much more than a way station to our next existence.
- Encouraging is, in actuality, instilling confidence in the lives of others, a necessity when preparing for war.

### Needed: Teammates from all walks of life

Here's your opportunity. As members of God's army and God's team, you have a responsibility to your fellow soldiers and teammates. That responsibility is to do whatever you can to assist them in overcoming their next obstacle in life. Teammates by definition are "a group of people with the same goals and intentions who work together to bring out the best in one another." And nothing does that like encouragement. This book constantly points out that people, all people, need to be encouraged. We need to be encouraged because God doesn't want us eking out our existence here on this planet; He wants us to flourish and become the overcomers He has called us to be. That can only happen when we join together His resources and use them liberally on each other. Just keep in mind, one of God's most abundant resources is encouragement.

**15**

# Don't Wait; Encourage Now

*But encourage one another daily.*
*(Hebrews 3:13)*

The saddest person has to be the one who is convinced his life doesn't matter. For someone to actually go on living each day believing they don't make a difference or that what they do doesn't really account for anything has to be one of the most depressing experiences there is.

Six years ago my brother-in-law David took his own life. He was certain his existence had no purpose. He had voiced many times to his sister (my wife, Michele) and to me that his life was insignificant. He obsessively compared himself, and his life, to those of others he deemed more successful and meaningful, and it caused him to become terribly depressed. In all truthfulness, the depression he was fighting was accelerated by the chemicals he used and the alcohol he drank in an effort to mask the pain.

As family members, we tried to validate him, but it was difficult. We found ourselves in a relentless battle with the power of his substance abuse. Tormented daily, Michele persistently attempted to reinforce in him the amount of value his life held. But we were family; we were supposed to tell him that, right?

As a pastor, I attempted to counsel him scripturally, but again, as his brother-in-law, I'm afraid it was merely expected that I would. There were more than a few times we experienced the agony of helplessness. Was there something else we could have done? That's a question we've asked ourselves more than once over the past six years. Second-guessing became something we did almost on a daily basis. I'm here to tell you, however, that God continues to free us from the guilt the devil wants us to shoulder over this tragedy. Praise and glory to God!

So what was the answer? What could have kept David from carrying his .22 caliber rifle out to his front porch and, at forty-nine years of age, ending his life? He was educated and intelligent, sensitive and caring. He held a good job and seemed to have a group of peers with whom he frequently associated. Was there anything *anyone* could have done? That's a question in which only God holds the answer.

One of the most heart-wrenching times came at his calling hours as our family greeted his friends and co-workers. It was amazing how many of those people shared stories of how David had, at one time of another, made a difference in their lives. We heard how kind he was, how he would constantly go out of his way to help them, how he took the time to listen and counsel them, how he would do small projects for them without any desire to be compensated, how he had such a great sense of humor.

After listening to all these people for two or three hours, our entire family was blown away. The question I wanted to ask every one of them: Did David know all of you felt this way about him? Did he know *any* of you felt this way about him? Did any of you ever tell him? What my family heard being shared that night, as we stood in front of his casket, was what he needed to be told every day of his life. But then, maybe he was being told and it didn't matter. Maybe the combination of drugs, alcohol and depression was just too overwhelming for any amount of encouragement to make a difference. But maybe, just maybe, there was a time when it would have mattered.

**Encourage when the opportunity presents itself**

My goal in sharing this very personal and tragic story isn't to heap guilt on those who knew David and maybe didn't reveal to him how they felt. I truly believe most had no idea of the extent of his depression. His sister and I didn't really know. Rather, my goal is to make all of us aware that there are Davids around us every day, some we know to be hurting and some of whom we have no clue.

The question I need to ask is: Should it really matter how badly someone is hurting before we offer to help? If we were to just go about our every day spreading encouragement in the opportunities presenting themselves, it's possible we could help prevent a tragedy like this from ever getting to such a degree. At the very least, in sharing with others how we feel about them, we'd still be making them feel better about themselves.

And how can that ever be a bad thing? The Word of God tells us to come to the aid of our enemy for goodness sakes.

*If your enemy is hungry, feed him; if he is thirsty,*
*give him something to drink.*
*(Romans 12:20)*

If this is how we are to treat those who are considered to be our enemy, how much more should we be doing for those who are our family members and friends? The truth is, if you know someone steeped in depression, it's probably going to take more than encouragement to pull them out. If you even think depression is involved, my advice is to pray, of course, but also to encourage your friend or loved one to seek professional help. Keep in mind though, encouragement when given regularly may prevent that someone from ever getting to the point of needing professional help.

**God is the God of hope!**
Maybe that hurting and depressed someone is you. Maybe you've convinced yourself that nobody cares. Maybe you have begun to believe you might be better off doing what my brother-in-law did and end your life. That is a lie from the pit of hell! Listen, regardless of how you may feel, you are the very possession of God Himself. Don't you dare allow the enemy of God to trespass anywhere on God's property, even in thought.

There are people who love and care about you, even if they may not be telling you. They might even be telling you, but because you're so focused on the things you are hurting from, you're unable to recognize the positive reinforcement others are offering.

My brother-in-law seemed to be fixated with looking at all the things other men his age had that he didn't have, like a wife and family, and he allowed those things to become his measurement of failure. If there is something that is sure to give you a sense of despair and a cause for you to want to give up on life, it is the addictive practice of desiring the things others have that you don't. In David's mind, every time his life didn't measure up to someone else's, it became just another brick of failure. When it got to the point of those bricks becoming just too heavy to carry, and he reached what he thought to be the point of no return, he then started down the slope of hopelessness.

Psychiatrists and counselors agree that hopelessness is the number one cause for people attempting suicide. More than divorce, more than health problems, more than poverty, hopelessness is seen by many as the last straw. True hopelessness gives no possible chance for anything to ever get better. I am here to tell you if there is one thing God wants us to know about Himself, it is that He is the God of Eternal Hope.

> *May our Lord Jesus Christ himself and God our Father, who*
> *loved us and by his grace gave us eternal encouragement*
> *and good hope, encourage your hearts and strengthen you in*
> *every good deed and word.*
> *(2 Thessalonians 2:16-17)*

As long as there is breath in our body, we have hope. You see, when there is breath in our body, we still have the opportunity to take our pain and anguish to God. And when God is given the reins of our distresses, there is no such thing as hopelessness. Turning our eyes to the Lord also takes them off the hopelessness of things, such as comparing our lives to the lives of others. God saw the destructive power this attitude possesses and went so far as to devote His tenth and final Commandment to it.

> *You shall not covet your neighbor's house. You shall not covet your*
> *neighbor's wife or his manservant or maidservant, his ox or donkey,*
> *or anything that belongs to your neighbor.*
> *(Exodus 20:17)*

### God is our one true Encourager

Waiting around for others to encourage us may take more patience than some of us can find. If there is one thing I've come to learn, it is that people, all people, will sooner or later let us down. It is the nature of people to do so. They don't want to; they don't mean to, they just do. However, I have also discovered that there is One who will never let us down. One who has never abandoned us, One who has never forsaken us. And while you and I may look at our lives from time to time and wonder "Where is God today?" I can without reservation assure you He is as close as we desire Him to be. Keep in mind, God doesn't go anywhere He isn't welcome. On the other hand, He goes everywhere He is invited.

If you see yourself anywhere in this discussion of hopelessness and depression and you've attempted unsuccessfully to pull yourself out, all is not lost. As a matter of fact, nothing is lost, certainly nothing of eternal value. Your job may have been taken from you or your spouse may have left you, yet you are still the personal possession of a loving merciful Father, the kind of Father who chooses to leave the ninety-nine while He goes to search for the one who's lost. If that one is you, and you see yourself as lost, go to God and tell Him how you feel; seek His counsel where the counsel of others has failed. Look to Him for the encouragement necessary to make your life whole again. He not only has an endless supply of it, He can't wait to give it away. It is my belief that He will begin to show you an incredible purpose for your life. And believe me, nothing can encourage you more than discovering your purpose.

## Remember...
- Share encouragement the moment you have the opportunity. Opportunities have a way of disappearing quickly.
- Don't wait for someone to be hurting before you affirm them. That hurt they're experiencing may have been avoided had others spoken to them the healing words of encouragement.
- If you're the one needing encouragement and think no one cares, just know that God not only cares, He also has an incredible purpose for your life.

## Ask to be led
Take a moment today in the presence of God and ask Him to lead you to someone who is in need of an encouraging word. It may be someone fighting hopelessness. If it is, ask God to give you the heart of an encourager, then step boldly into His role for you as the giver of hope.

*May the God of hope fill you with all joy and peace as you*
*trust in him, so that you may overflow with hope by the*
*power of the Holy Spirit.*
*(Romans 15:13)*

# 16

# Encouragement: Use It or Lose It

*Every good and perfect gift is from above, coming
down from the Father of the Heavenly lights
who does not change like shifting shadows.
(James 1:17)*

E ncouragement is a good and perfect gift from God to His people.
Now, gifts are not the same as wages. Wages, we earn; gifts, we
receive out of love and appreciation. By giving us gifts, God is demon-
strating His unconditional love and appreciation to His children. God
doesn't love us because we're good little boys and girls. God does not
appreciate us because we follow His commands and act holy. That's one of
the most difficult concepts for people to understand, even for those within
the Church.

Somewhere we got the idea that we can earn the favor of God. We
can't. God's favor is a gift. He and only He determines who receives His
gifts and no amount of sacrifice or saintly living can earn nary a one.
And for us even to consider that somehow we deserve God's precious
gifts is absurd. Therefore, it should be assumed that nothing we can do
on our own, regardless of how good or religious it appears, will bring us
the gift of encouragement. That's what makes receiving His encourage-
ment and any other gift He has chosen to give us so special. It's knowing
they're all based solely on one thing: His love. Now, if there's one thing
I've discovered about God and His endowment of gifts, it's that He's
endowed us for a purpose. That purpose is clear according to the apostle
Paul in Romans 12:8:

*If it (the gift from God to us) is encouraging,*
*let him encourage.*

I know Paul and the other New Testament writers wrote in the structure of that day, but I believe if they had felt a little more freed up, verse eight would have read like this.

*If you got it, use it!*
*(RLE, Revised Lamport Edition)*

You see, God does not send us gifts just to send us gifts. Everything God does has a purpose, and unless I've missed the better part of His philosophy for life, that purpose has everything to do with improving the lives of other people. Nothing can improve lives any more than you and I empowering them with words of affirmation. So, let those words of affirmation go forth and accomplish what God has intended. Let's speak them every opportunity we get.

By His omniscience, God determines which children should receive which gift, and upon bestowing those gifts, He fully expects them to be put to use. That concept is made quite clear in the Parable of the Talents in Matthew 25:14-29. When you read the following portion of Scripture, keep in mind that while the literal meaning of *talent* was a unit of coinage, the spiritual connotation is that of a godly gift or ability.

*"Again, it will be like a man going on a journey, who called his servants and entrusted his property to them. To one he gave five talents of money, to another two talents, and to another one talent, each according to his ability. Then he went on his journey. The man who had received the five talents went at once and put his money to work and gained five more. So also, the one with the two talents gained two more. But the man who had received the one talent went off, dug a hole in the ground and hid his master's money.*

*"After a long time the master of those servants returned and settled accounts with them. The man who had received the five talents brought the other five. 'Master,' he said, 'you entrusted me with five talents. See, I have gained five more.'*

*"His master replied, 'Well done, good and faithful servant! You have been faithful with a few things. I will put you in charge of many things. Come and share your master's happiness!'*

*"The man with the two talents also came. 'Master,' he said, 'you entrusted me with two talents; see, I have gained two more.'*

*"His master replied, 'Well done, good and faithful servant! You have been faithful with a few things; I will put you in charge of many things. Come and share your master's happiness!'*

*"Then the man who had received the one talent came. 'Master,' he said, 'I knew that you are a hard man, harvesting where you have not sown and gathering where you have not scattered seed. So I was afraid and went out and hid your talent in the ground. See, here is what belongs to you.'*

*"His master replied, 'You wicked, lazy servant! So you knew that I harvest where I have not sown and gather where I have not scattered seed? Well then, you should have put my money on deposit with the bankers, so that when I returned I would have received it back with interest.*

*"Take the talent from him and give it to the one who has the ten talents. For everyone who has will be given more, and he will have an abundance. Whoever does not have, even what he has will be taken from him."*

### The number is not what's important

Jesus spoke in parables for various reasons. One of the more significant reasons I believe was to cause those hearing His parables to spend time examining their significance and applying them to their lives. Relevance and application has always been the key to unlocking the Word of God. Jesus had a way of personalizing every parable by including our lives in each one. For example, everyone can identify with one of the three servants in this parable. Let's say you were the one given the five talents. What's that? You don't feel as though you were given five? Okay then, maybe you were the recipient of two talents. Huh? Not so sure about the two? Then you were the one who was given one. Now before you go off wondering why others may have been given more, keep in mind the portion of your talent isn't all that important. As a matter of fact, the amount of your talent is probably the least important aspect of the story. However, in our worldly but limited thinking, we're always emphasizing numbers; the bigger the better, right?

God doesn't put anywhere near the emphasis on numbers that we do (read about Gideon in Judges 7). What needs to be emphasized, however, is the fact that the talents were God-given, which means whatever the measure, it was enough. God doesn't miscalculate. He never shortchanges us nor does He overwhelm us. The true theme of this parable is found in your understanding of what it is you can do with your measure of talent that will bless the heart of your Master, despite the amount you've been given.

**Give it away and there will be more**

If we are to learn anything at all from the words of Jesus, the answer is to see how quickly we can give away our talents. Two of the servants in this parable were blessed by their master. They were blessed, not for how much they had but for how much they *invested*. What can't get lost here is the fact they invested *all* of it. And because they invested all of what they had been given, there is for us a very specific and significant lesson in this parable. The one essential and undeniable truth we learn from these first two servants is that when we give away what God has given to us, there will always be abundantly more made available.

It might sound cliché, yet no truer words can be spoken: "It's impossible to outgive God." But unfortunately, that's not how we live. A large part of our lives are spent hoarding what we do have and sulking over what we don't have, regardless of how much we find ourselves with. That attitude is the antithesis of this parable. There was only one servant who hoarded what he had, and it doesn't take a theologian to see how he was *rewarded* for his incredible selfishness.

Amazingly, we often waste so much time on evaluating and counting our talents, there's no time left to invest any of them. I bet if we were truly honest here, most of us would agree that we spend considerably more time out of our day wondering why we don't have as much as the next guy and so little time being grateful for the measure we've been given. Listen, the bottom line is this: If it's more you want, then follow the formula of this parable. God has given us a simple blueprint for obtaining more. Through the efforts of the servants, we see that more is obtained only one way: by giving away whatever we already have. That practice may not make sense to the world but it's a principle of God that has been time-tested. Either way, it's always better by far to be thankful for the measure we have than it is going around moping about what we think we need. Thinking we need anything outside of what God has already provided is a monumental waste of time. The following Scripture reinforces to us that God's measure to us is always sufficient.

*And my God will meet all your needs according to his glorious riches in Christ Jesus. (Philippians 4:19)*

The word *all* in this verse is not ambiguous in any way. God satisfies our insufficiencies, all of our insufficiencies. Whether it was the monetary support Paul needed from the first-century churches as referenced in this Philippians Scripture, or the strength God promises to give His children when we're experiencing weakness, God is sufficient!

**Put the gift on display**

Whatever your measure of encouragement, display it. Not, *display it* as in some act of pride, but *display it* by giving it away. Give it away every day. I think we can all agree after reading this parable, the last thing we want to do with our gift from God is to go out and bury it somewhere.

When it came to displaying gifts, my mom was the best. I used to bring home all kinds of horrendous things I made at Cub Scouts or summer camp. I remember the time I brought home an apple with cloves pushed into it. You were supposed to hang it up or set it out in the kitchen to make the air smell better (this was way before aerosols and air wicks and such.) Well, not only did my mom hang that apple up in our kitchen, she also made a point of showing it to everyone who came over, saying "Look what my son made me!" or "Did you see the beautiful apple Reid gave me?" Eventually the thing shriveled up to the size of a golf ball. I think my dad got tired of looking at it and threw it away, but my point is, when we make a big deal out of a gift someone gives us, it brings pleasure to the giver of that gift.

I don't think we can please God more than by putting to use (displaying) the gifts He gives us. My mother's grateful attitude and resulting action after receiving one of my gifts caused me to want to bring home something different for her every day. She never looked at that apple and wondered why Lance King's mom got two of them. No, she appreciated what she had been given and demonstrated her thankful heart by immediately putting it to use. Are you making the connection here?

The final words in the parable say, "Take the talent from him and give it to the one who has the ten talents" [in other words the one with ten talents is the one who displayed his gift and used it the way God desired]. "For everyone who has will be given more and he will have an abundance."

I have to believe God is no different from any of us when it comes to seeing His gifts displayed; and I have to believe His gift of encouragement has to be one of His favorites because of the way it makes His children feel. God has given us life and it's His desire we live it in fullness. When His children are being encouraged, they are experiencing a portion of that fullness. How pleased God must be as He watches members of His family make the effort to encourage one other. I'm sure He has to be grinning ear to ear every time words of affirmation are spoken, thinking to Himself, "Now they're getting it!"

### Remember...
- A gift is something we're given, not something we earn.
- Gift givers want nothing more than to see their gifts being displayed (used).
- Knowing your gift has been given to you by God also lets you know the amount is always sufficient.

### What are you doing with your talents?
So, what are you doing with your talents? Are you one who tends to see what others have and wish for more, or do you take what you've been given and out of gratefulness give it away? It's important to get your eyes off what the rest of the world does with their talents. Look instead at the reason you have what you have. Chances are, your talents have been given to you for one reason, to begin investing them into the lives of others. Investing is such an accurate term to describe the giving away of your talents, because in each and every case where talents have been given out, they always return with interest.

# 17

# Hiding from Encouragement

*Nothing in all creation is hidden from God's sight.*
*Everything is uncovered and laid bare before the*
*eyes of him to whom we must give account.*
*(Hebrews 4:13)*

You would think we'd learn sooner or later, wouldn't you? If not from our own attempts to conceal things from God, then from all the Sunday school classes we attended which should have convinced us that keeping things from God is never a good thing. Adam, Cain, Jonah, Ananias and Sapphira, to name just a few biblical personalities, have taught us how futile it is to think we can keep secrets from God. Yet with all this experience, with all of this proof, with all of this prior knowledge, we still hold out that there are some things we're better off leaving in the closet. When will we discover once and for all that issues, something everyone deals with, need to be faced head-on? But before we can think about facing them head-on, we must first acknowledge they exist.

God has been unbelievably good to me. I can honestly say He has enabled me to live more than my share of lifetimes. I have been blessed to have been a teacher for thirty-seven years, which has afforded me thousands of relationships. I have had the blessing of planting a church and the added blessing of serving it for the last eleven years, all the while enjoying the loving relationships provided by that experience. I have also coached four varsity sports that have given me the opportunity to establish a good deal more relationships with young people and their families.

Now you would think if there was anything I would know anything about, it would be people. And while I certainly don't profess to know all that much, there is one thing I can tell you about all people. They have issues. Not as in things they have to change to become better people issues, but rather things they have difficulty dealing with on a daily basis issues. I remember a number of years ago a term became popular that described certain families who didn't measure up to the so-called *normal* family. If it seemed as though the issues they were dealing with were excessive or severe, counselors and psychologists were quick to label them "dysfunctional." After my many years of dealing with the problems of children, athletes, and families, both in and out of church, I have to honestly say I have yet to find a family that is *functional*. Suffice it to say, I'm still looking for the family that hasn't had their share of issues. Now the severity of those issues can change from family to family, but each of them has their own set of problems they have to come to terms with.

**Encouragement is needed where problems exist**

The characteristic that separates certain families from one another is how they deal with their problems. Some families pretend that problems are something only their neighbors have. According to them, they never have issues; and if you were to visit their home you would more than likely be seeing a smoke screen of the real family. Never wanting to admit there are times they feel as though they're coming apart at the seams, their actual day-to-day family life resembles what looks like reruns from *Leave it to Beaver*. As Mother June attempts to sweep everything under the proverbial rug (wearing her heels and pearls), the Cleaver family pretends that life's trials, difficulties, and anxieties can be overcome simply with a word of wisdom from Father Ward.

While the show always had a good moral theme and taught a weekly lesson on ethics, it hardly portrayed today's reality. Reality says that all families have real issues facing them, issues that can't be dealt with by sending a child to his room in an effort to *think it over*. While I can't recall the Cleavers ever having to deal with any *major* issues, at least they always dealt with the ones they faced. Not so today. There are far too many families who are more interested in how others perceive them than they are in dealing with their problems. The truth be told, these are the families who seem to struggle more than most. Their goal is to portray the perfect home, which we know doesn't exist, so things that suggest their home may not be perfect are just ignored.

Refusing to acknowledge and then deal with the daily difficulties of life will present only one thing: more difficulties. When we purposely ignore the day-to-day problems all families face, there will never be a need to encourage one another. Encouragement is needed where problems exist. If you never admit you're struggling, if I'm never aware there are serious issues going on in your life, then how can I ever encourage you in dealing with those issues?

I've discovered through my associations with the so-called *perfect families*, their household tone is usually one of weariness and discouragement. The family is so busy and so worn out attempting to hide their problems from others, there's never any time or energy left to come alongside and support one another. Dealing with problems can be painful, no doubt, but unless those problems are brought to the surface and dealt with, there can never be any healing. Without healing, wounds and scars caused by everyday living are left open and susceptible to infection, which can be a lot more painful than admitting they exist and facing them.

**Sharing our issues give others hope**

People who don't cover up issues, but instead readily admit they're burdened with, well, burdens, leave plenty of opportunity for family and friends to come alongside and encourage them through those issues. Generally the first step in overcoming a problem is by admitting, "I've got a problem on my hands." Environments where trials and issues are openly dealt with present ample opportunities for encouragement. The more people who are made aware of your situation, the more openings there are for prayer and support. This is not to say all laundry should be aired in public; there are some things that should be kept within the family setting. However, if you have others whom you trust, maybe a home church group or members of a Bible study, their added prayer and support can go a long way in helping you triumph over those problems.

Admitting we have issues can also play a major role in assisting others. When people hear there are families and individuals out there dealing with the same junk in their lives as they are, that can be a great source of encouragement. Not only will it give them confidence to open up about their problems, but also it will be reassuring to them as they discover they're not out there treading water alone.

Michele and I experienced this first-hand a number of years ago after we began holding a Bible study in our home. About six months or so into the study, one young mother mentioned how surprised she was to learn of all the issues the Lamports had to deal with. Until the Bible study, she had known us only through the fellowship of church and had assumed we didn't have to deal with the type of issues we acknowledged were a part of our lives. She admitted she was sorry to know we were experiencing such things; however it also gave her hope to know her family wasn't any different from most *normal* families.

### Sharing opens the door for healing

To see what hiding issues can ultimately result in, let's look at the biblical story of Ananias and Sapphira and the first-century Church. Jesus had just gone back to the Father following His forty days on earth as the Resurrection and the Life. The disciples, along with all the other believers, were meeting together in an effort to encourage each other in their faith. The Church was in its beginning stage of organization, and all the believers, in an attempt to establish unity in the body, made a decision to sell their property and pool their money.

Ananias and his wife, Sapphira, two people who were a part of that body, had some major issues going on in their lives they were reluctant to share. If you would like to refresh your memory or read over the specifics, the story is found in Acts 5:1-11. After Ananias and Sapphira contributed money they received from selling some property, they were brought before the leaders of the church where they attempted to falsely take credit for donating more money to the church than what they actually gave. The truth was, they were giving but a portion of their real estate transaction while claiming they had bequeathed all of it. Their desire to conceal part of that payment (greed), coupled with their desire to be praised for their false generosity (pride), proved to be a fatal mistake. In addition to lying, the couple obviously had some serious issues they still needed to address.

The truth of the matter was, there were probably more than just a few within that early church dealing with some of the same issues themselves. Had Ananias and Sapphira brought those issues to the surface and confessed them before their brothers and sisters in the Lord, they would have had the benefit of knowing they weren't alone. Knowing that others were dealing with the same thoughts would have opened the door for healing. Not only that, but by revealing their pride and greed, it would have given the rest of the church the opportunity to provide the prayer and encouragement needed to deal with their sin. By not bringing their sin to the surface, they were inviting the devil to gain a stronger foothold in their lives, and that will always result in disaster. They would have done well to take heed to James' words:

> *Therefore confess your sins to each other and pray*
> *for each other so that you may be healed."*
> *(James5:16)*

## Once hope enters, healing can begin

There are a number of reasons James says we are to confess to one another. Confession is the first step to repentance, something Mark 1:4 says is needed before forgiveness can take place. Confession also works to keep each of us accountable to one another. By sharing my weaknesses and my propensity to sin with a trusting brother in the Lord, I am allowing him opportunities to pray for me. I'm also giving him access to areas of my life where he can join with me to spiritually battle things I just can't battle alone. By confessing and sharing my sins, I'm opening myself up to be encouraged in areas I've never permitted others the right of entry.

By keeping the things we're struggling with a secret, we're providing the devil opportunities to convince us how futile it is to fight against him. (When we battle alone, our opponent knows he can attack our vulnerable areas with things such as fear and shame over past failures.) The devil is relentless. We get so discouraged and feel so defeated that we find ourselves tossing up our hands and saying, "What's the use?" When someone is of that mindset, that's where encouragement can play a vital role. When we're only hearing the words of the enemy resounding in our head, it isn't long before we become convinced of what he's saying.

"You can't win; you're not strong enough."

"You don't have what it takes."

"There's definitely something wrong with you."

"Too bad no one else has to deal with these same issues."

Even though they are blatant lies, by being isolated and alone, those accusations begin to sound like truth. But when others are made aware of our situation, they can begin to encourage us with the *truth* from God's Word:

- *All things are possible with God (Matthew 10:27).*
- *Never will I leave you never will I forsake you (Hebrews 13:5).*
- *In all things God works for the good of those who love Him (Romans 8:28).*
- *In this world you will have trouble, but take heart I have overcome this world (John 16:33).*

The Word of God brings immediate aid to a discouraged heart and allows us to see hope in our situation. Once hope enters the picture, healing can begin.

> *And we rejoice in the hope of the glory of God. Not only so, but we*
> *also rejoice in the sufferings, for we know that suffering produces*
> *perseverance; perseverance, character; and character hope. And*
> *hope does not disappoint us, because God has poured out his love*
> *into our hearts by the Holy Spirit, whom he has given us.*
> *(Romans 5:2-4)*

### Just follow the Word of God

I'm discovering more and more one of the most important roles we have as spiritual brothers and sisters is to speak the Word of God into one another. Nothing can be as encouraging as hearing Scripture fill our hearts and our minds. The key is giving others more and more opportunities for doing just that. Before that can become reality, however, it's going to take people who are willing to open up and expose the weaknesses in their lives. That's not easily done. It takes trust.

Trusting that others will encourage us and not judge us is paramount to opening up and confessing our need for help. If you want to be an encourager of others, it's essential to first get rid of your propensity to judge them. Let me also make clear that giving advice when it's not asked for is a form of judgment. By encouraging others with Scripture rather than advice, we are assuredly avoiding the judgmental spirit most of us have become so gifted in demonstrating. It's really quite simple if we just follow the Word of God.

There are reasons we can find Scripture on virtually every page of the Bible telling us how we can be an encouragement to one other; and yet there is not one Scripture telling us to how to judge one another. That's why God has provided for one Judge, but millions of encouragers. All we have to do is stop attempting to fix everyone's problems and instead just make ourselves available and become the encourager we're called to be. The more we do, the more others will be persuaded to stop hiding their issues and start sharing them; that's when the healing begins. And let me tell you, where there is healing, there is an incredible amount of joy waiting in the wings. When God delivers one of His children from bondage, or removes from someone a heavy burden that has been draining the life and energy from them, or when He chooses to perform an emotional, physical or spiritual healing, the elation found in those experiences is so overwhelming, it's nearly impossible to keep quiet about it. Besides, the last thing we should be doing after a supernatural movement of God is to keep quiet; to God goes the glory!

We need to be sharing our experiences with all those who have been praying for us and encouraging us so they themselves can be encouraged. That's why testimony is such an important part of our faith. When I hear the difference my prayers and support have made in someone's life, I'm invigorated to participate in more of those opportunities. I'm convinced that one area where we as Christians fall short is in celebrating the mercies and blessings of God. We'll stand and cheer like fanatics when our favorite team scores a touchdown, but where is that same excitement when a brother or sister in the Lord shares a victory in their life? God is to be celebrated in every circumstance, especially when that circumstance includes overcoming an obstacle in life. When we have the privilege of witnessing one of those events, our enthusiasm should be uncontainable.

*We will shout for joy when you are victorious*
*and will lift up our banners in the name of our God.*
*(Psalm 20:5)*

There's another reason we are to share our victory; it's to encourage all those who are struggling with similar situations not to give up. They have to know there is some degree of hope for them. People just need to see there is light at the end of the tunnel in order to keep on; but more importantly they need to know just who that light is.

*Jesus spoke...I am the light of the world.*
*Whoever follows me will never walk in darkness,*
*but will have the light of life.*
*(John 8:12).*

Whatever you do, don't keep God's healings a secret. Others need to hear the source of your joy. They need to know that same joy can be theirs as well. There are many lessons we can learn in all this, and each one is based upon our willingness to quit hiding our problems and instead begin sharing them with the encouragers God puts all around us. When we do that, our chances of overcoming those burdens will not only increase significantly, but we'll be also providing others the opportunity to come alongside us and demonstrate the love of Christ.

*Remember...*
- Reality says that all families have issues to deal with, and the families who bring them out in the open have a much better chance of experiencing healing.
- It's crucial to share our victories over issues we have to deal with in life, if for no other reason than to encourage all those who are struggling with similar situations to know there is hope.
- By encouraging others with Scripture rather than offering them advice, we will assuredly avoid the judgmental spirit most of us have become so gifted in demonstrating.

### *Are you serious about experiencing healing?*

Everyone has problems. That isn't even debatable. What is debatable is how you deal with those problems. You can hide them and pretend they don't exist, or you can share them and allow others to assist you through them with encouragement and support.

I hope you like challenges, because I've got one for you. If in the past you've been inclined to keep everything to yourself, I'd like for you to try something, that is, if you're serious about experiencing true healing. Identify someone you trust with your life. It doesn't have to be a close friend or a family member; it could be someone at church, possibly someone older or wiser than you. Ask them if it would be alright for you to share something personal, something that has caused you anguish or maybe even pain. It could possibly be something you're not sure if you've been forgiven for. In the midst of your discussion, if they don't suggest it, ask them to pray for you. Chances are, the moment you open up and confess what it is that has been weighing you down, a burden will lift and healing will begin.

# 18

# Quit Competing and Start Encouraging

*We do not dare to classify or compare ourselves*
*with some who commend themselves.*
*When they measure themselves by themselves and*
*compare themselves with themselves,*
*they are not wise.*
*(2 Corinthians 10:12)*

Having experienced competition on a field of play as both an athlete and a coach, I can unequivocally say that the vast majority of people are highly competitive. People like to win, and while there's nothing scripturally wrong with wanting to win, too many people carry it to an obsessive degree. It's as if they'll let nothing stand in the way of them getting their way. That's an attitude we've come to expect from the world, but the truth is, it's not a whole lot different within the body of Christ.

The win-at-all-costs attitude doesn't bode well with the Christian philosophy that says the welfare of other people is far more important than personal records or achievement. We're taught this and we know this, but the problem is getting our lifestyle to follow. Getting people to agree to it on Sunday morning isn't the problem; the dilemma occurs once we leave church and go back into the world where everyone around us has the dog-eat-dog attitude. We Christians find ourselves getting caught up in the competition, and often our defense is that we do it to survive.

It's really no surprise, everything we take from the world and incorporate into our lives has us compromising our values. We can attempt to justify our worldly competitiveness as much as we want, but the bottom line is this: It conflicts with the Word of God. The corporate handbook tells us to use people as ladder rungs while God's handbook tells us to untie their sandals and wash their feet. The world gives seminars on the menagerie of ways there are to ascend above the next guy; God calls us to reach down as far as we have to in order to help the guy up. As Christians who operate in the world, we find ourselves faced with a dilemma: Do we follow the motto of the world or do we follow the Word of God? There is no third option. I wish there were. If someone could write a book containing acceptable third options, there's no doubt in my mind it would instantly become a best-seller. If third options were an option, there would be no need for Jesus to have said:

> *Dear friends, do not be surprised at the painful trial*
> *you are suffering...However, if you suffer as (for being)*
> *a Christian, do not be ashamed, but praise God that*
> *you bear that name.*
> *( 1 Peter 4:12,16)*

Regardless of how difficult it is, regardless of what others think about us, regardless of how soon or if ever we get that corner office, God calls us to encourage one another and build one another up. The truth be told, there's a powerful spirit of worldly competition among God's people that God never intended for His body of believers. It has no place within the family of God. In Chapter 4 of this book, this worldly competition was identified as *selfishness*; this chapter suggests another word that equally defines it. You can masquerade it as competitiveness, being high-spirited or having spunk, or you can just call it what it is: *jealousy.*

> *You are still worldly...there is jealousy and*
> *quarreling among you.*
> *( 1 Corinthians 3:3)*

## Jealousy is a powerful spirit

The apostle Paul never minced words. He had received reports about the Church in Corinth. The believers there were living worldly and spiritually immature lives. One of the issues of immaturity he addressed as their pastor was the issue of jealousy. The believers in Corinth needed to be reminded, and as brothers and sisters in the Lord today, we need to be reminded as well that in the family of God there's no such thing as sibling rivalries.

Our Father gives all His children equal attention. We shouldn't be competing against one another; we should be *serving* one another. Jealousy is an enemy of God that calls us out constantly. As Christians, we find ourselves fighting that battle every day. We've been engrained with worldly competition since the beginning of time. With some help from the serpent, Adam and Eve permitted the spirit of pride to enter the Garden and blind them to the generosity of God. They permitted the devil an opening where he convinced them that no one else should have anything they don't have, not even God. The serpent seized the opportunity and made it about competition.

> *You will not surely die, the serpent said to the woman. For*
> *God knows that when you eat of it your eyes will be opened,*
> *and you will be like God, knowing good and evil.*
> *(Genesis 3:4-5)*

Now we all know what happened when Eve believed the lie of Satan. However, the world of trouble that followed all could have been prevented had Adam and Eve responded a little differently to the temptation of the devil. They could have said something like, "You're not as smart as you think you are, serpent. We have the freedom to enjoy all of these trees in the garden. Look around you, devil. There's an endless supply of fruit. We've been given blessings left and right. Who cares if there's one tree we can't eat from? There's plenty here for everyone."

God encouraged the first family by enabling them to have everything, everything but one thing, that is. And it was that one thing the devil succeeded in getting them to focus on and obsess over. The thought that someone else had one more thing than they had was the heel the devil attacked. There could have been fifty-billion trees at the first couple's disposal, but knowing there was someone who had fifty-billion and one, even though that someone was God, proved to be too much of a temptation to ignore. Jealousy isn't something everyone sooner or later outgrows; the spirit of jealousy is a powerful spirit, and thousands of years of human history haven't changed its intensity one bit.

**Jealousy is a battle that cannot be won by human effort**

As a result of the Garden experience, we've become such competitive and jealous people. If there is something someone else has that we don't have, never mind the endless supply of fruit at our disposal; we tend to obsess over that one thing that's not ours. That's the spirit of jealousy digging its talons into our flesh. Don't think for one minute this is something new. The apostle Paul allowed himself to become transparent in his letter to the Romans not only to help us identify this spirit when it surfaces but also to offer us some much needed encouragement.

> *When I want to do good, evil is right there with me. For in my inner being I delight in God's law; but I see another law at work in the members of my body, waging war against the law of my mind and making me a prisoner of the law of sin at work within my members. What a wretched man I am! Who will rescue me from this body of death? [Now for the encouragement.] Thanks be to God through Jesus Christ our Lord!*
> *(Romans 7:21-25)*

If we don't immediately respond by taking authority over that spirit through the enablement of God and reminding ourselves to be thankful of all the blessings we do have, we're going to constantly fight the battle of comparing ourselves to, and competing with, everyone else; and believe me, that's a war we don't want to launch.

Now you'd think as believers we'd know better, but unfortunately I see God's Church fighting this war all the time: youth pastors hustling for other churched children in an effort to boost their numbers; territorial preachers resistant of coordinating events with other local bodies for fear of losing sheep; denominations criticizing other denominations; and the list goes on. This worldly attitude of strengthening the local church at any expense has indeed weakened the corporate Body of Christ.

There are many things we can do to combat and bring to defeat this jealous spirit that has infiltrated the Church. One of the most effective ways is through encouragement. Encouraging those around you, especially those you're jealous of, is a way of defeating the harassing spirit of jealousy. The last thing your flesh wants to do is encourage someone it's feeling jealous about; as a matter of fact, you'll find yourself wanting to criticize them a whole lot more than encourage them. The first step in overcoming jealousy is to first identify that it's indeed jealousy you're experiencing. For without first identifying what you're feeling, you'll never be able to take the necessary steps to defeat it.

*So I say, live by the Spirit, and you will not gratify the*
*desires of the sinful nature...the acts of the sinful nature are*
*obvious...jealousy...selfish ambition.*
*(Galatians 5:16,19,20)*

Jealousy is a battle that cannot be won by human effort; that spirit is just too entrenched within our nature. It must be drawn out and defeated by the Spirit of God. The way in which we do that is the same way we defeat all enemies of God, by consciously overcoming evil with good. Only God is good, and when we allow His good virtues to replace our selfish sinful virtues, we're going to find ourselves on the road to victory.

When you're feeling jealous, begin immediately to meditate on the intimate relationship you have with the Lord Jesus. He saved you, which is deeply personal; He desired you out of all the people on the face of the earth and welcomed you into His glorious kingdom. Feelings of jealousy have a hard time existing where contentment and thankfulness dwell. After all, how can you still be jealous after coming into the realization that you are granted the riches of heaven? When you're into one of your jealous modes, allow God's mercy to overwhelm you and remind you of what His incredible grace has afforded you. Jealous? What is there to be jealous about when we're guaranteed the eldest son's share of the inheritance? Knowledge is understanding not only *who* we are, but more importantly, *whose* we are; and realizing we belong to Christ is to realize there isn't anything we don't have.

*I pray... that the eyes of your heart may be enlightened in order*
*that you may know...the riches of his glorious inheritance.*
*(Ephesians 1:18)*

### Jealousy will not walk away on its own
God desires to enlighten our hearts. He wants us to see and appreciate all we have in Him. When we truly evaluate everything with which God has blessed us, an attitude of gratefulness overwhelms us. We have the benefit of knowing, through the Word of God that all that belongs to Christ also belongs to us. The world doesn't possess this same gratefulness because the world doesn't have this knowledge. And yet, knowing all this, we still choose to compare ourselves with other people as if we're

competing with them for our Father's favor. Those who constantly permit the spirit of jealousy to torment them by thinking this life is about who has the most stuff will find themselves bound to that battle every day; because every day they will discover someone else who appears to have more, or someone else whose life seems a little better, or someone else who might have it a little easier.

Jealousy is a spirit that will not walk away on its own; you must take authority over it. One of the steps to help you take back that control is by submitting to the daily practice of encouraging others. When we're encouraging others, we are actually overcoming the urge to compare ourselves with them. By desiring for those around us to be blessed, and then blessing them with words of affirmation, we'll find there isn't time for senseless jealousy. But if the desire to compare yourself with someone else should arise, just be obedient to the Word of God and compare yourself with Jesus.

> *You're attitude should be the same as that of Christ Jesus:*
> *Who...made himself nothing...taking the very nature*
> *of a servant.*
> *(Philippians 2:5-7)*

## Our flesh never has our best interest at heart

If anyone deserved it all, it was Jesus. Jesus, however, constantly made it about others. Did the spirit of jealousy harass Him? That's a good question, one you can ask Him someday, but for today we are to take His lead and assume the nature of a servant. When we willingly serve and aren't made to serve out of obligation or tradition, but instead choose to do so on our own, it makes a world of difference. Jesus willingly served. He "*made himself nothing*" and that was his first step of making others something. Jesus chose to put His needs and desires on hold in order to meet the needs of those around Him. Eating became something He did after others were fed; resting came once the last person was prayed for; and Jesus was constantly making it about others by handing out encouragement everywhere He went.

Granted we're not Jesus, but there are many things Jesus did we can emulate, and one is to encourage others. Voiding our lives of jealous desire and destructive comparative thinking is a matter of taking back control of our lives from our flesh. Our flesh never has our best interest at heart; it has its own best interest at heart. The flesh is constantly after one thing and one thing only: making itself feel good.

Our flesh works hard to convince us that instead of seeking to encourage others and making them feel good, we're the ones who deserve to be encouraged; we're the ones others should be validating. The amazing thing about following the Word of God for our lives is, when we're obedient and unconcerned about getting our due, God finds a way of fulfilling every desire we have.

> *But seek first his kingdom and his righteousness,*
> *and all these things will be given to you as well.*
> *(Matthew 6:33)*

Go out and encourage others regardless of the fight your flesh puts up, and you'll be amazed at the amount of blessings that come your way. My guess is, you'll be having so much fun spending time esteeming those around you, there won't be time left over for you to spend on hosting any "Why can't I have what others have?" parties.

## Remember...
- There's a powerful spirit of worldly competition among God's people that God never intended for His body of believers. It has no place within the family of God.
- The first step in overcoming jealousy is to first identify that it's indeed jealousy you're experiencing.
- Encouraging those around you is an excellent way of defeating the harassing spirit of jealousy.

### *How do you define the word* competitive?
Before we can begin to take back more control from our flesh, it's important to recognize things as they are. One is the difference between being competitive and being jealous. We'll probably need to redefine the word *competitive*. As mentioned earlier, just being competitive isn't necessarily a bad thing. As followers of Christ we'd better learn to compete; it takes more than a little competitive spirit to overcome this world and all its trials and tribulations. However, *competitive* becomes *jealousy* the moment resentment enters the picture. If and when you begin to experience resentment, you must distinguish it as such and place it under the control of God's Holy Spirit. If you don't, it will seek to torment you with an attitude of bitterness; and we all know how unattractive bitterness can be. When we're actively engaged in esteeming and encouraging others, bitterness has no room to breathe.

**Part 4**

# Techniques for Encouraging

*Whether you're already an accomplished encourager
or seeking to become one, here are some tips and
techniques you may find useful as you go about
your life uplifting others.*

# 19

# Encouraging With Our
# Mouths Closed

*You hear, O Lord, the desire of the afflicted;*
*you encourage them, and you listen to their cry.*
*(Psalm 10:17)*

Encouragement can come to us and be delivered in any number of ways. Some of the best encouragement comes through esteeming words and relating examples from our lives, but it's not limited to those two areas. True encouragement is anything said or done to enhance the lives of others. It need not be complicated or earth-shattering. Some of the best encouragers I know rarely, if ever, open their mouths. One thing they are, however, are great listeners.

When we take the time to listen to someone, it can be for them an extremely important source of encouragement. Even in our silence we can validate someone else's life. By merely listening when others need to talk, we are telling them, "I'm here for you; what you have to say is important and worthy of my time." People need that, and I'm sorry to say I'm guilty of not offering it as often as I should.

### Encouragement needs engagement

The area of my life where I constantly fall short is encouraging my wife, Michele, by being a good listener. If just being physically present constituted encouraging, I might be okay, but in reality there can be no encouragement without engagement. Engagement doesn't necessarily mean conversation either. Engagement simply means *to involve oneself.*

Michele desires me to involve myself when she needs to talk. She doesn't need me to fix her problems or offer my advice; she does, however, need me to listen attentively. I believe most men are by nature dreadful listeners. We simply don't see the benefit in merely listening; to us it's a lot like going shopping and not buying anything. However, it doesn't get us off the hook just because listening skills weren't included as part of our nature package. By nature, I mean something which comes naturally; and since listening doesn't seem to come naturally to most men, it's something we're going to have to work at.

It's the same as being good conversationalists. I'm going to go out on a limb here and say I believe most men, in general, make poor conversationalists. Again, I'm not saying this to excuse us men in any way; I'm just letting some wives know that their husbands aren't the only ones going out of their way to avoid conversation. I'm also attempting to encourage some men who might think they're the only ones who would rather scrape the rust off a bumper than to listen attentively and exchange verbiage with their wives when they feel the need to talk.

Men, a bit of advice here: When confronted by your wife for miserably failing as a partner of conversation, you should avoid at all costs attempts to justify it with comebacks like, "That is not how God made me" or "I'm just not wired like that." It's never a good idea to place even partial blame on God. Plus, to say it was His intent to make us this way is unfounded. I've searched the Scriptures extensively and found no verses informing us that gender was a factor in God determining who was to inherit the "gift" of conversation and who wasn't.

It is interesting, however, to read in God's Word;

> *Women should remain silent in the churches.*
> *They are not allowed to speak.*
> *(1 Corinthians 14:34)*

The question is, regarding this Scripture, were women being instructed to keep quiet in church in order for them to wait until they had the full attention of their husbands at home, or was Paul inferring that there had to be at least one place on earth where men could go to get a break from the "joy" of listening? I'm going to give you the freedom to interpret that Scripture as the Lord leads!

**Lack of communication falls on the shoulders of us men**

After fifty-nine years on this planet, I have come to know that very few men, relatively close to my age, enjoy talking on the phone. Consequently, I know of very few women between the ages of, let's say, eighteen months and a hundred and thirteen, who aren't passionate about phone conversations. This common enthusiasm the vast majority of women seem to possess has enabled most of them to evolve the skill of conversation into an art form. This has all been reinforced to me by observing two of my children growing up as they conversed on the phone. My daughter Katie, who from the time she was nine, talked as though every phone call was a conference call. I swear there had to be four or five people on the other line because it would be virtually impossible for one person to process the amount of information she was giving in such a short period of time. A typical conversation of hers went something like this:

"…I-talked-to-Lyndra-who-told-Tiffany-that-Barry-won't-see-her-anymore-because-she-made-fun-of-his-jeans-    you-know-what-jeans-the-ones-with-the-high-waist-and-straight-legs-of-course-he-didn't-get-them-at-Abercrombie-they-don't-sell-that-stuff-guess-who-I-saw-in-Abercrombie-though-that's-right-Kevin-and-he-wasn't-with-Shannon-he-was-with-some-girl-from-Columbus-which-means-Shannon-is-back-with-Tyler…."

All of that was said between two breaths while Katie was doing her nails and watching "Iron Chef." You can't tell me that's not some kind of genetic gift.

Then there's my son Reid. I'd like to say his telephone skills have evolved a great deal over the past fifteen or twenty years, but alas, such is not the case. His conversations on the telephone seem to demonstrate a cognitive form of delayed speech patterns. He is currently working on his master's degree and I can only thank God it's not in oral communication. A typical phone conversation of his goes something like this:

"What?…………………shut up…………………no way……………… dude you're lying………………uh…uh……………I dunno…………… maybe………………I'll call you later."

I only hope he's not talking to one of his professors. It's remarkable. The differences are astounding! Is it any wonder that, generally speaking, women make the best listeners? That doesn't get us off the hook though, men. What it does mean is, we have to make more of an effort, a concerted effort. I purposely injected a little humor in depicting the natural differences between men and women, but the truth is, there are far too many marriages in trouble today and that's not humorous in the least bit. It breaks God's heart, and I believe many of the problems stem from a lack of communication. That lack of communication almost always falls directly on the shoulders of us men. Too often it's we who brush aside our wives' need for someone to talk to or someone who will just listen. As men, we like to think, "There's value in fixing things; there's value in giving advice; there's value in working things out. But to just listen; where is the value in that?" The truth is, the value is in our relationship with our wife.

### Don't downplay your role as a listener

Wherever there's a need to be a listener, there is great value in fulfilling that need. It doesn't matter if it's high on our priority list or not. If it's what our wives need, then it should be a high priority of ours as well. So often, listening is exactly what our wives need, and to know their husbands care enough about them to really listen esteems them. It encourages them. If nothing else, they find security in knowing their husband is making the effort to involve himself in something that is important to them.

Don't downplay your role as a listener. Make the effort, men; God commands us to unconditionally love our wives. Unconditional means you are to love your wife under every condition. If she needs to talk, love her by talking with her. If she needs you to listen, love her by listening to her. The bottom line is, there are thousands of ways to love her; one of the most important is to be there when she needs you. (For more on encouraging our wives, see the chapter Encouraging Our Spouses.)

Encouraging with our mouths closed carries over to other areas of our lives as well. Whether we're in the workplace, school or out with a friend, it's important to become sensitive to the needs of those we're with. Sometimes those needs involve listening. Whenever a friend, classmate, or co-worker decides to *open up* and become vulnerable by sharing something personal, the least we can do is listen. If they want our opinion, they'll ask us; and if they ask, go ahead and tell them what you think. Just remember, the most important thing you can do is be there for them as they share.

### It's really all about the person

Feeling ignored is one of the worst feelings there is. It causes the person being ignored to feel as though their life and all aspects of their life are unimportant and irrelevant. The last thing we want to do is ignore someone who trusts us enough to expose some significant part of their life.

Whether or not what they have to say holds great significance to us isn't the question. It's really all about the person. If we care about them, then we should care about what's important to them.

When someone is talking to you, look them in the eye. This non-verbal cue not only tells them you're engaged in what they're saying, but also it forces you to give them your attention, and giving someone your undivided attention is a great source of encouraging with your mouth closed. To encourage people by listening doesn't take a master's degree in counseling; it may, however, take a little assistance from the Master Himself. It's easy to envision Christ sitting down with someone and giving them His undivided attention. The Bible doesn't give us a lot of dialogue between Jesus and other people, but anyone who has studied the life of Christ knows the value He placed on relationships. It's one of the reasons He still desires to have a relationship with each one of us. Jesus genuinely cares for all His disciples; therefore He deeply values what we have to say.

Try becoming an encourager through listening. I'm convinced it will not only bless the hearts of others, but it will give incredible meaning to your life as well.

### Remember...
- Feeling ignored is one of the worst feelings there is.
- Wherever there's a need for someone to listen, there is great value in fulfilling that need.
- True encouragement is anything said or done to enhance the lives of others.

### Be someone's source of inspiration
Quite often those around us don't need our advice, or our suggestions; they crave our attention. There are many times when just being *an attentive ear* can encourage someone else. When others know they have our full attention, that in itself is an endorsement of their importance to us. As people see their importance to us, it will work to elevate their self-esteem, and they become validated. To know we can become a source of inspiration to others, simply by engaging ourselves in their lives, is an exciting realization. It's also exciting to realize we don't always have to have the answers in order to *be there* for someone.

### Author's note:
I'm including a note of praise here to show you how our God is such a confirming God. Recently I attended a Bible study in the home of one of

our church leaders. As the pastor, I try to attend the weekly studies our various fellowship groups hold as often as I can. While this particular study was winding down, the group shared with me an idea for a new ministry they wanted to launch. Amazingly enough they're calling it a *listening ministry*. When they told me, I couldn't believe it. I was just finishing up this particular chapter, which I had not previously shared with any of them, and yet our line of thinking was identical.

Not only were we thinking along the same lines, but also the group and I both felt strongly enough to do something about it. Now some would call that a coincidence. I rather think it was God prompting us and then validating what we're doing; and believe me, when God does that in your life, it's an amazing feeling. It seems their goal in this listening ministry is to visit a local assisted-care facility once a week and invest quality time with the residents by simply listening to them. They feel by sitting down and spending time attending to what the residents have to say, they will be providing much needed encouragement. Their goal isn't to preach, fix problems or offer advice; they're just lead to go and listen. Personally, I can't think of a better way of encouraging someone with our mouths closed.

## 20

# Encouraging by Way of Omission

*A man of knowledge uses words with restraint.*
*(Proverbs 17:27)*

While up on my ladder doing some gutter repair recently, I noticed someone walking by the house. When I turned to see if I could recognize who it was, the person stopped in front of my garage and seemed to be staring at my front lawn. It was a lady I had never seen before. Not knowing why she was looking at my house, I decided to climb down to see if she needed help with anything. Before I had a chance to speak, she looked at me and said, "Your landscaping is beautiful."

Now I'm not one to ever think of my landscaping as anything of the beautiful caliber, so I did what anyone would do. I thanked her. The truth is, I enthusiastically thanked her. My wife and I have worked hard to make the outside of our house look nice, but I still never saw it as all that special. Returning to the ladder, I thought, "That lady doesn't know me; she really could have just admired the landscaping without saying anything and continued her walk." But the reality was, she didn't, and because this lady didn't keep her admiration of our lawn to herself but choose instead to share it, Michele and I were the benefactors of her encouragement.

In the midst of replacing my ladder in the garage, I began to look around at all the clutter caused from six months of stacking stuff and using our garage as a storehouse for everything we didn't want in the basement. I have to tell you, the sight of it was almost overwhelming. I wondered, as I always do in the spring, how I let it get this bad. I also wondered how that lady who had just inspired me by telling me how nice our landscaping looked failed to remark about the devastation in my garage. No one would have blamed her had she finished her assessment of my property by saying something like, "Your landscaping is beautiful, however, you might want to keep that garage door down." But she didn't. The eyesore our garage was had to be just as apparent as our Japanese Cherry and Blooming Dogwood, but she chose to speak only words that uplifted my spirit and esteemed me. Had she mentioned the state of the garage, even in a joking manner, her encouragement concerning the yard would have been nullified. She would have been accurate had she included something negative about the garage, but then I would have walked away feeling defeated rather than uplifted.

### When encouraging, stick to encouraging

This little encounter got me wondering about the times I have said something encouraging to someone only to nullify my words by attaching something negative. I believe that happens more than we think. For some reason, we feel as though it's okay to mention something less than positive after we have just exhorted someone, something like: "Hey, Chloe, that dress looks great on you. I can hardly tell you've gained weight."

Okay, that was a little obvious. How about this one?

"Son, I am very proud of the way you reacted to that other boy's behavior. Now if you can just do that at home and stop acting like a baby with your sisters, you'll be on to something."

Or try this:

"Honey, I really appreciate your cleaning up after supper; if only I could get you to do that without me having to remind you."

There's a lesson to be learned here. When encouraging, stick to encouraging! It might not be easy, but if your intent is to lift up and validate someone, then this is vital. Sometimes we want to mask our true intent, so we think by saying something positive first, the blow that's to come might be lessened. That's not encouraging; that's sugarcoating a rebuke. I'm not trying to say we should never rebuke someone; I'm just saying it shouldn't be on the coattails of a word of encouragement.

There are going to be times when we have to share something of a less-than-encouraging nature. Even the truth itself can be discouraging at times, however, the time for sharing it should not be immediately following a word or two of exhortation. The main reason you're speaking encouragement in the first place is to esteem someone. Tagging that validation with sarcasm or scorn does nothing to esteem them. As a matter of fact, it tends to negate anything of a positive nature you may have told them.

**Parents should be especially careful**

Parents are probably as guilty as anyone when it comes to this practice. I can think back on a number of times I corrected my children by starting out with something positive. I thought by beginning with an affirmation they'd be more inclined to receive my admonition. My thought process has since changed. The reason it's changed is because that philosophy has never worked with me.

Let's say Michele is attempting to *train* me to keep my shoes away from the entry into our house. If she starts out by telling me how much she appreciates my cleaning up the family room and then moves immediately to, "I just wish I could get you to do something about your shoes," I will have remembered nothing about the family room comment. My attitude will be affected by the one negative remark. Now if it works that way with me, an adult who knows his shoes shouldn't be left in front of the doorway, it's definitely going to work that way with a child. I'm not saying we don't have the right or even the responsibility to teach our children by correcting and training them; I am saying there is a time and a place for doing it.

If our children are misbehaving or being disobedient, they need to be told; most of the time they need to be told right then and there. We certainly don't exhort our children following inappropriate behavior. Why then would we rebuke them following appropriate behavior? It only makes sense. Do whatever you have to do as a parent to instruct and correct your child as to what is acceptable and what isn't. I'm talking about the times when our children, or others, do something or say something worthy of praise. Go ahead and, by all means, commend them. But then, leave it alone. You may have something negative you've wanted to share with them for some time, but you've been putting it off because it might be a little uncomfortable. Don't think by buffering it with encouragement, after they've done something praiseworthy, you'll be softening the blow any, because you won't. The only thing you'll be doing by that practice is smothering the encouragement.

**It's really about self-discipline**

I believe it comes down to motive, motive and another little thing we call self-control. The first thing to look for then is the intent of the potential encourager. If the intent is to validate someone, then just validate. But if the true intent is to correct or attempt to manipulate the behavior of another person, don't use the charade of encouragement to do so. Again, there is nothing inherently wrong with correcting or rebuking the negative or inappropriate actions of others, especially if it is done with a loving spirit. If you're a parent, that process becomes a regular part of your life. When doing it, though, don't initiate your correction by bringing up something you should have positively reinforced your child for at an earlier time.

Attempting to plug in a quick praise or affirmation before a rebuke will only serve to waste an important encouraging moment. If you have squandered an opportunity to validate your child, or someone else, just be patient (isn't it a virtue we all possess?) and wait until the next appropriate time. Then take advantage of it. It will certainly carry a lot more meaning when it stands by itself.

Often it's our lack of self-discipline that's responsible for our inability to hold our tongue when we know we should. No matter how long we have followed God's advice in our lives, holding our tongue is one of the most challenging of all commands. In all likelihood, part of it is our nature and part of it has to do with the infrequency with which we encourage. We're like perpetual novices when it comes to encouraging. We do it with such infrequency, it's almost like a brand-new experience every time we lift up another person. There's an easy cure for that. Start by encouraging someone every chance you get, and while you'll never reach perfection, it won't take long before you begin to hone your skills as an encourager and eliminate the mistakes that come from inexperience and lack of self-control.

*For God did not give us a spirit of timidity, but a spirit*
*of power, of love and of self- discipline.*
*(2 Timothy 1:7)*

If someone has done something that warrants an encouraging word from you and it's your desire for them to continue that practice, it only makes sense that you tell them you appreciate what they've done. How else are they going to know that what they've done is something you're grateful for? It really boils down to common sense. Reward positive behavior. The true purpose for encouragement is to reinforce, support, give confidence and motivate, among a whole slew of other things. As you speak your words of encouragement, let them go forth and accomplish what they're intended to accomplish. Just be disciplined enough to omit your less than inspiring comments until a more appropriate time. Who knows, after blessing the person's heart through encouragement often enough, maybe there won't be as much need to correct them in the future.

**Remember...**
- Don't attempt to buffer a word of correction by beginning with a word of encouragement. It won't work. The encouragee will only focus on the correction, and the affirmation will most likely be lost.
- Inexperience and lack of self-discipline are the two main reasons people tag their encouragement with a rebuke. When encouraging, stick to encouraging.
- Parents, be especially careful when attempting to train your child. If they do something to warrant a verbal high-five, end it there. Don't throw in a quick word of sarcasm for good measure.

**Work at it**

Encouraging by way of omission is going to take a lot of practice, especially if you're as gifted as I am in tossing in quick, sarcastic barbs. The best measuring stick is to reverse the roles. Think how you would feel if someone had just encouraged you and then followed it up with a discouraging remark, regardless of how accurate it might be. If your intent is to have the person walk away from you esteemed, fight the urge to attach a less than positive addendum.

# 21

# Encouraging by Example

*Similarly, encourage the young men to be self-controlled.*
*In everything set them an example by doing what is good.*
*(Titus 2:6-7)*

There's a philosophy when teaching others that says the best way for someone else to learn is by demonstrating the lesson before them. In other words, since most people are visual learners, let them see how it's done. That always works best for me unless I'm attempting to learn something about plumbing. Then it doesn't matter. But take anything else, and I'm much better off when I can see someone else doing it.

Encouragement is no exception. One of the most effective ways of encouraging someone who is going through a difficult time is by example. When others can see you dealing with problems similar to theirs, especially when they observe you surviving those problems, it can be a great source of encouragement. Not everyone is capable of encouraging by example; it takes people who are going through, or have already gone through difficult situations others can relate to. Telling someone who is experiencing pressure and anxiety in their life how they should be living their life is not quite the same as allowing them to see just how successfully you deal with those same issues. While sharing your crisis experiences will probably take more than a little courage, the benefit to others can be immeasurable.

**Share the wounds**

Let's say I am attempting to raise my children as a single parent. It is a foregone conclusion there are going to be times when I get overwhelmed.

Times when I think, "No way am I going to be able to do this." Worry begins to rush in and I am quickly convinced no one else on the planet has to deal with what I'm dealing with. To me, my problems seem matchless and unsolvable. Here is where the value of *encouraging by example* can be invaluable.

You come along, a single parent yourself, and as you begin hearing the trials and tribulations I'm now going through, you realize that here is someone else who is exactly where you were five or ten years ago. Now you could tell me, "I feel your pain," or "I'll be sure to pray for you," and while I might appreciate your comments because you did validate my situation and offer some words of encouragement, my discouragement is walking away with me because you haven't given me any reason to be hopeful that my present situation will ever get better.

When I mentioned a moment ago that it might take more than a little courage on your part to *encourage by example*, here is what I mean. For you to relate to my hurt and pain, you're going to have to become a little transparent. You'll have to open up your life to me, and that can be a difficult thing, especially when I don't really know your story. You may have kept a number of things from your single-parenting days a secret, especially the times that caused you the most pain and grief. It's very possible that you haven't shared those times with anyone because of the wounds they may open up. However, the wounds are the very thing I want to hear about, because where I am at the moment; wounds are something I can relate to. I need to know my pain is relative to your pain so that your healing can be for me a source of optimism. I need to know, from someone who has gone through what I'm now going through, that one day it's going to be okay.

### There's purpose in your trial

As much as we may feel as though our problems are unique unto themselves and no one else could possibly be experiencing what we're experiencing, keep in mind there are six-billion people on this planet at any given time. Odds are, there are more than a few who have gone through the same matchless and unsolvable experiences as you. Granted, some may have thrown in the towel, but there are plenty of others who have persevered and come out on the other side holding the flag of victory. While the process of obtaining victory may have been difficult and quite challenging, just knowing others have overcome similar trials and are here to tell about it can give us the inspiration to do likewise. These are the people

God can use in powerful ways to impact the lives of others by offering *encouragement through example.*

Something extremely important to bear in mind here is that the flag-holder, the one standing on the victory platform looking back on what was once thought of as insurmountable obstacles, might be you, and if it is, don't you dare keep your story a secret. There was a distinct purpose for going through what you went through. It may not have been to write a book about it, but I can say with a strong degree of certainty, neither was it to hide it from the world. By sharing your story, you can give hope to those who feel hopeless.

Here are some powerful words of *encouragement by example*:

- "I was right there exactly where you are and let me tell you how it can be done."
- "If I can do it, so can you. Here's how I was able to do it...."
- "There were times when I swore I wasn't going to make it through another day, but I'm here as living proof to share what enabled me to overcome the pain."

You don't need to be a great communicator or have the character of a saint, in reality you just need to be someone with a heart set on helping people overcome their trials of life. Those willing to *encourage by example* are people like you and me who have experienced difficult and seemingly unsolvable situations but persevered through those challenging times by the hand of God. They are ordinary people who have overcome the extraordinary through the strength of the Lord and the encouragement of others. Amazingly enough, more often than not they'll tell you their lives today are better for having experienced what they did.

**Become that lifeline of hope**

Divorce. Guilt. Bankruptcy. Addiction. Depression. Trials such as these, which are so rampant in our society today, are paralyzing the children of God by binding them to anxiety and fear. Most of their fear is triggered by the thought of never being able to overcome their trial, whatever it might be. They desperately need some measure of hope. When people begin thinking their problems are hopeless, all life and energy they once possessed gets drained out of them. They become so absorbed in the negative aspects of their situation that the joy and peace Christ wants all of His children to reap from this life become for them a non-entity.

There are countless numbers of people without hope, struggling just to keep their head above water. By sharing your story of victory, you could be serving as their lifeline. Just hearing how you persevered and knowing there are others who have experienced the same thing and survived is one of our greatest sources of encouragement. As I mentioned earlier, however, it's not going to be an easy thing to do; it's going to be painful, and all pain, even old pain, hurts. It's here where you're going to need the help of God's power to carry it out. The apostle Paul knew about pain and he knew about hurts. As a matter of fact, he was tormented by a "thorn in his flesh," constantly.

*Three times I pleaded with the Lord to take it away from me.*
*But he said to me, "My grace is sufficient for you, for*
*my power is made perfect in weakness."*
*(2 Corinthians 12:8-9)*

The first step in experiencing God's power for your life is to first come to the understanding that you desperately need it. It will take someone willing to admit they're just too weak to live this life on their own. Paul learned through the encouragement of God that if he would just acknowledge his weaknesses and stop trying to sustain himself during times of trials and tribulation, God would then make His power available to him. Too often, people in pain come to the realization that they're not going to make it under their own strength, but regrettably they begin looking for that strength in all the wrong places. Stories abound of families and relationships being destroyed over a hurting member looking for strength and thinking they have found it in drugs or alcohol. In every one of these cases, the family member discovers, rather quickly, such things only enhance their pain and compound their problems.

A ton of hurt can be saved by looking first to the omnipotence of God rather than to the fleeting remedies offered by man. Something I have found that helps to diminish the pain of old hurt is to use it as a source of comfort and inspiration for someone else. By sharing your story with others and seeing firsthand the release of pain from their life can work to accelerate your own healing process.

I believe the best part of *encouragement by example* is coming into an awareness that the God of the Universe may be using you to encourage and bring healing to one of His hurting children. That realization is pretty staggering. What also needs to be considered a possibility is that God sustained you through your trial for you to assist others through their times of trial. If that's the case, then regard it an honor.

> *Consider it pure joy, my brothers, whenever you face trials of*
> *many kinds, because you know that the testing of your faith*
> *develops perseverance.*
> *(James 1:2-3)*

The joy James speaks about is not the *pain* of going through the trials. The joy is what's waiting for those who persevere. Don't ever underestimate the importance of sharing your story with those going through similar situations. Through your *encouraging by example*, you are supplying people with hope. Hope enables us to go on. Hope gives us a reason to live. As Christians, we know the source of all hope is ultimately found in the Lord Almighty.

> *Blessed is he…whose hope is in the Lord his God.*
> *(Psalm 146:5)*

**Personal encouragement is powerful**

We all need to realize that our Lord, in whose hope we live, can assign us to be His vessel of hope. There are web sites and chat rooms all over the internet serving as places for people to go to read about others suffering from similar problems and situations. This can be, and is, a great source of encouragement. My advice, though, is never to skip opportunities God may be presenting you to share your story face to face, waiting instead to post it on-line. Posting your story may be less stressful and less painful than sharing it personally; it will not, however, carry the intimacy or the power of a personal testimony. If God is blessing you with opportunities to assist Him in comforting hurting souls one on one, He will also enable you with the necessary power and strength required to carry them out.

> *Praise be to the Lord…because He has come…*
> *to enable us to serve Him without fear.*
> *(Luke 1:68,74)*

While posting or writing your story gives it the prospect of reaching the eyes of many, your encouragement is enhanced greatly when others can *see* the healing in your eyes, *hear* the healing in your voice and *feel* the healing in your touch. Emotional and spiritual bonding cannot be experienced on the internet.

Quite often, when devastating times appear in our lives, the first question we ask is, "Why, God, did this happen? It makes no sense." You see no visible benefit to anyone whatsoever. Maybe you looked to Scripture in an effort to try and understand why. Possibly someone led you to Romans chapter eight.

> *And we know that in all things God works for the good of*
> *those who love him, who have been*
> *called according to his purpose.*
> *(Romans 8:28)*

Maybe you read this Scripture or others like it and experienced little or no comfort. "My good?" you questioned, "How can this possibly be for my good?" You still may be struggling with the application of that verse, as we did for so long when attempting to apply it to the suicide of Michele's brother. However, the thought occurred to us that maybe, just maybe, we were to share our pain and our heartache with others who have gone through similar experiences and let them know not only can there be healing, but also actual joy on the other side. Many times it comes down to choice. We can choose to believe God's Word, "In all things God works for the good of those who love him," or choose to believe He doesn't. It's quite possible "the good" Paul speaks about can be found in encouraging others who have gone or are going through similar experiences.

The best part is, we have the choice and the God-given power that goes with it to encourage others, and in so doing glorify the Lord of glory. We also have the option to ignore others, bury our hurt and believe that nothing good could ever come from our painful situations. What a mistake that would be. The beauty is, it's our choice to reach out to others. And that choice could bring not only a great sense of comfort and healing to someone, but amazingly to our own lives as well.

Maybe you never thought about sharing your story. Maybe in your mind no one could possibly benefit from the experiences you have gone through or are still going through. Don't be so quick to judge. Even if you deem your circumstances to be unique unto yourself, I encourage you to share the fact that after experiencing what you have, here you are, alive and well! People need to see and know they can one day be where you are. You may not even have it all together; your healing may be only partially complete. It doesn't matter. You have given someone else hope, and whatever you do, don't ever underestimate the cathartic power found in hope.

*We continually remember before our God and Father your*
*work produced by faith, your labor prompted by love, and your*
*endurance inspired by hope in our Lord Jesus Christ.*
*(1 Thessalonians 1:3)*

### Remember...
- The most effective *encouragers by example* are those who are going through or have gone through some of life's most difficult struggles and are willing to share how God has sustained them.
- Don't ever pass up opportunities to share your story if you think others may benefit.
- Becoming transparent is the first step in assisting others in overcoming the trials and difficulties of life.

### Get serious
Okay, just how serious are you about helping to heal the wounds life has sustained on your fellow man? Serious enough to do something about it? Serious enough to use your own life experiences as examples and give God's children a measure of hope? If you are, and I pray you are, don't be too surprised if you find your own healing moving to another level.

# 22

# Encouraging Through Rejoicing

*Rejoice with those who rejoice; mourn with those who mourn.*
*(Romans 12:15)*

Why do we go to funerals, calling hours, wakes? If we truly stop to think about it, it's not for the dearly departed. I have a hunch they're not overly concerned with who's there. Actually, it's worry over such things as what people think that may very well help contribute to putting us in our caskets prematurely. However, once our physical bodies are placed in one, we're free from worrying about what others think.

We should be aware that our greatest benefit in going to funerals and calling hours is to "mourn with those who mourn," just as Romans 12:15 says. Our purpose in attending such functions is to provide emotional and spiritual support for the family and to let those left behind know we're hurting with them and praying for them. In other words, our presence at funerals is a way of encouraging one another.

Now, many people will probably tell you they go to such things to pay their respects to the dearly departed, say their last good-byes, so to speak. And while that seems honorable enough and well-intentioned by those who do, personally, I would much rather have my friends paying their respects to me when I can most appreciate it, say, when I am still among the living and breathing.

While mourning with one another does have merit and value, and there are definite times when it provides comfort and encouragement to those who are experiencing grief and sorrow, it's still painful to go through. If most of us were given the option of mourning with someone or rejoicing with them, it's a pretty safe bet we'd choose rejoicing. It's because there's joy in rejoicing, hence, re(joy)cing. When we rejoice, it's like we're celebrating, and celebrations are a lot more fun than memorial services.

**Seize the opportunities we have to rejoice**

What I hope to accomplish in this chapter is not to downplay the times we must mourn with those who mourn, implying that somehow they're not as significant as the times we can rejoice with those who rejoice. The Bible tells us there are going to be painful times we'll have to experience in this world, and having loved ones around hurting right along with us is crucial in assisting us through such ordeals. As a matter of fact, having others mourn with us might be the source of healing we need to help us eventually move past the pain.

My goal is simply to make each one of us conscious of just how many opportunities we have to rejoice with one another, and to make us aware of how important it is to seize every one of those times. It would be nice if this world offered us only opportunities to rejoice, however, if there's one thing we continue to learn about this temporary and fleeting world, it's how unsympathetic and harsh it really is. In becoming an encourager, it's important to see both mourning and rejoicing as ways of encouraging others just as Paul points out in the opening Scripture verse. Providing comfort and encouragement to our fellow man, regardless of whether it's through rejoicing or mourning, is both a privilege and a responsibility.

*If you have any encouragement from being united with Christ,*
*if any comfort from his love... then make my joy complete by*
*being like-minded.*
*(Philippians 2:1-2)*

**It's going to take getting involved**

I heard someone say once, you can tell how well a person has lived his life by counting the number of people at his funeral. And while that means of measuring someone's life may have some merit, it becomes a little depressing to think all those people are there to encourage by way of mourning. If I had my way, I would institute rejoicing celebrations as a way of balancing out the number of funerals that are held, places where friends and family can go to join loved ones who have a reason to rejoice.

There should be times set aside for people to join celebrators by expressing joy over an exciting moment in their life. I know we have birthday parties, retirement celebrations, baby showers and the like, but there are so many other reasons for which *American Greetings* has not made a card, times when we can come alongside our brothers and sisters and just be excited for them.

I'm really talking here about everyday victories that are important to people. And while holding a celebration for every one of them may be unrealistic, it shouldn't stop us from hosting our own personal celebrations for them. But to do that, it's going to take us becoming actively involved in the lives of other people. The trade-off, however, will be well worth the effort. If we were to ask people which they would rather do, rejoice or mourn, it's a foregone conclusion they're going to choose to rejoice.

There are going to be times though when the option is not ours, times when rejoicing isn't appropriate and mourning with them is the only means of providing encouragement. As Christ followers, we have to be able to provide for others *whatever* is needed, *whenever* it's needed. Identifying with others in their joys and in their sorrows is not just a Christian's privilege, it's also our responsibility. I don't believe most of us are aware of the regularity with which we pass up opportunities to pay our respects to the living.

## It's like giving them a verbal hug

Recently I had the opportunity to encourage a number of my students after report cards came out. Even though a couple of the students were in a state of mourning, the majority of my encouraging came by way of rejoicing with them. The students who worked hard and earned good grades were genuinely excited to show me their report cards. When they did, I had a choice in how I was going to react. I could compliment them as I have been inclined to do in the past, or rejoice with them by joining in their excitement. It would have been the difference of either patting them on the head and saying "Nice job" or hugging them and exclaiming "Wow, I couldn't be more proud of you!"

This particular time I chose to hug the snot out of them, and the results were startling. Each student I rejoiced with was noticeably encouraged by my reaction. I also wrote a note of encouragement on their report card, and they couldn't wait to show it to the other teachers. Now you might be thinking, "Come on, Reid, you're talking about report cards. How do they fit in with this discussion of funerals and such?"

First of all, I'm not talking about report cards or funerals; I'm talking about people and what's important to them. Those who desire to become true encouragers identify what's important to others, and allow those same things to become important to them. It can be something as simple as report cards or as significant as the birth of a baby. Encouragers committed to encouraging purposely seek out daily opportunities to come alongside others and rejoice with them. Waiting until something such as a funeral has taken place, where we're almost forced to say something of comfort, does not constitute being an encourager.

I'm learning that rejoicing with others has less to do with what they're rejoicing about and everything to do with just being excited for the person. God's Word doesn't say rejoice *only* with those who truly have something worthy about which to rejoice. It says, if someone else is rejoicing, so should you. Regardless of how we feel about it, Jesus tells us it's something we should do.

> *Suppose one of you has a hundred sheep and loses one of them.*
> *Does he not leave the ninety-nine in the open country and go*
> *after the lost sheep until he finds it? And when he finds it he*
> *joyfully puts it on his shoulders and goes home. Then he calls his*
> *friends and neighbors together and says, "Rejoice with me;*
> *I have found my lost sheep."*
> *(Luke 15:4-6)*

Now, you can be someone who says, "It's one smelly sheep, for crying out loud, what's the big deal; you still have ninety-nine," or you can become a person of encouragement by rejoicing over the obvious *big deal* it is to them.

### It always comes back to love

Opportunities abound every day where we have the chance to "rejoice with those who rejoice." Far too often we pass on those chances because to us it's no big deal. If we keep passing on those opportunities long enough, the next thing we know, our only option for encouraging them will be to "mourn with those who mourn." Life is way too short not to seize the opportunities we have to rejoice when given the chance.

By making it your goal to rejoice with others when they are rejoicing, regardless of the basis for their joy, you will discover how much it affects your relationships. You will become someone they desire to be around. By providing motivation and inspiration, they'll begin to see you as you were created to be, a person truly concerned about enhancing the lives of others. In other words, you'll be modeling the life of Jesus.

*Each of you should look not only to your own interests,*
*but also to the interests of others.*
*You're attitude should be the same as that of Christ Jesus.*
*(Philippians 2:4)*

Jesus was obviously someone others were attracted to. No one else could *pick someone up* like Jesus. His time was spent helping others discover the purpose for their lives. That purpose, we learn over and over again through Scripture, is to love one another. It always comes back to love, doesn't it? We are to love one another in every way possible. Jesus did. One such way is being excited (rejoicing) with them when they are excited.

The painting of Jesus I love most is the one where His head is tilted back a bit and He's fully engaged in laughter. I personally believe He loved to laugh. So often we portray Jesus as this stoic and somber, always serious, individual who didn't have time for such things as belly laughing. Come on, God created us with a sense of humor. I have no trouble whatsoever envisioning Jesus joining His friends in an occasional chuckle or two. And I can only bet that some of those laughs were a result of His merely being happy over his friends being happy.

I'm ashamed to say, I have passed up way too many occasions where I should have been joining my wife, my children or my friends in their times of rejoicing, but instead chose to act indifferent because the things about which they were rejoicing weren't all that important to me. I've missed the boat far too long. And that's about to stop. I am committed to encourage those around me by rejoicing with them regardless of the source of their joy. If they're excited about something, I will be as well.

*Remember...*
- If our goal is to provide *whatever* our fellow man needs *whenever* he needs it, it's going to take us becoming actively involved with people and their lives.
- If we pass on opportunities to "rejoice with those who rejoice," we may find our only means of encouragement is by way of "mourning with those who mourn."
- Don't let someone's source of joy hold you back from rejoicing with them, regardless of how unimportant it may seem to you. If they're excited, you should be too.

### Keep in mind

Acting indifferent towards something that's a big deal to someone we love is selfish and uncharacteristic of Christ. It's important to understand that we're not just talking about events; we're talking about people and the things that are important to them. When someone else finds joy in something you don't, demonstrate a little unconditional love for them. Take your eyes off the source and put them on the person; I'm positive that is something Jesus would have chosen to do.

# 23

# Encouraging Through
# the Power of God

*Share with God's people who are in need.*
*Practice hospitality.*
*(Romans 12:13)*

In 1991, my family and I attended an FCA (Fellowship of Christian Athletes) camp on the campus of Albion College in Albion, Michigan. It was a multi-sport camp where high school students came to receive solid fundamental coaching in their sport of choice, centered in a Christian environment. I had been serving my high school as an FCA huddle leader for the previous five years, and attended a camp each summer with my family.

At Albion, I served as a member of its football coaching staff and led a group of coaches in a Bible study. The week was fairly structured, although there were a good many opportunities for staff to engage campers in social or spiritual conversations, and vice versa. I remember thinking how much I enjoyed talking football and exchanging philosophies with all the different coaches. Outside of that, nothing really jumped out at me; I felt as though it was a fairly routine camp.

Not too long ago, I received a letter from one of the campers who was there at Albion, a little more than nineteen years ago. Apparently, he and I had a dialogue that was both intense and quite significant. I would like to be able to say I remember this young man quite vividly and the conversation we had like it was yesterday (although I'm at the moment trying to remember what it was my wife asked me to do before she got home from work this afternoon); but the truth is, I vaguely remember him or our conversation.

Here is that letter:

*Pastor Lamport,*

*I hope this letter has reached the correct person. I attended an FCA camp in Albion, Michigan in 1991. A person by the name of Reid Lamport, which a Google search brought up you as the most likely Reid Lamport, was absolutely instrumental in bringing me to Christ. I want to thank you.*

*I've always been a questioner. I went to church, but could never fully embrace Jesus, God, the Bible, or religion as fact. It didn't gel with my analytical, scientific mind. I really wanted to accept Christ but too many intellectual roadblocks kept my heart and mind disconnected. The way you handled my doubt and me has become a model to me for how to respect-fully interact with my own students and children.*

*On Wednesday evening of our one week camp, you brought me out to the front steps and said, "Jeff, you have a lot of questions. I want to give you the opportunity to ask all of them. If it takes all hours or days, that's fine. I cannot promise I'll be able to answer them all, but hit me with every single question you have."*

*In eighteen years, no one had ever had the patience to say that. It was always placate and deflect. Now, as a teacher myself, I understand why, but back then, I was ecstatic to have someone sit with me and let me fire all the questions I had stored up. For over three hours, we sat and talked on the front concrete steps of the chapel. I asked every nagging question hin-dering my belief and acceptance. You were excellent in both your patience and Biblical knowledge. At the end of the marathon question session, I full heartedly and without reservation, accepted Jesus Christ into my mind and my life.*

*Just so you know, I went on to lead a Bible study in my high school after that. I received my bachelor's of science and eventually a master's of multi-disciplinary science. My wife and I were youth leaders in our church for years. I continue to teach math and science at an alternative high school in the Detroit area where the opportunities to talk one on one with students about the big issues they face abound. I tell you this because those three hours out of your life changed me forever and His kingdom has been advanced over and over again because you taught me the power of patiently listening to a questioning person. The youth in our church, my school, our Bible study, and my home (we have two wonderful children) have all benefitted from those three hours you gave me.*

*For years, I carried your card around in my wallet intent on someday letting you know how you've changed my life. Eighteen years is too long, but I did want you to know I will forever remember your respect, patience, knowledge, skill, and Christ's love and example you showed me.*

*Respectfully,*
*Jeff*

**No one else but God can change lives**

Upon reading this letter and after succumbing to tears, I was immediately and profoundly encouraged. It reinforced for me my purpose for being on this planet. It was like a fresh wave of God came over me and energized my spirit. I wanted to run out and find other inquisitive teenagers and begin answering their questions. His letter became the subject of one of my sermons, and more than a few people commented how much they were moved by it. As a matter of fact, it was his letter that helped to structure the writing of this book.

That's how it's supposed to work, this encouraging thing. When our only goal is to share the love of Christ, our acts have a way of returning, not only to us as a blessing, but to everyone who hears. Now I have to be honest and tell you my first thought after opening Jeff's letter was, does he have the right person? Something that life-altering and I really don't remember it, how can that be? What did I say to him that changed him so? As I began quizzing myself further about this encounter, the Spirit of the Lord spoke into my heart, "You didn't say anything, Reid; it was I. Those were My words not yours." When that thought began to sink in, I realized God had used me to bring a child of His into the Kingdom. That's the amazing part. It was God, and it had to be; no one else but God can change lives like that. Second Corinthians says it best:

> *But we have this treasure in jars of clay to show that this all-surpassing power is from God and not from us.*
> *(2 Corinthians 4:7)*

Now I knew back there in Albion that God is the one who brings about change in someone, but I wasn't thinking that, and because I wasn't thinking that and should have been, it convicted me. I became instantly humbled; first for thinking, even for a minute, that I had the answers to all of Jeff's questions. Then, when the second wave of humility hit me, I was on my knees for realizing the God of the Universe chose to use me in such a profound way. When I truly understood my role in this whole thing, I became even more encouraged. Nothing is more humbling, or more encouraging, than to come to the realization that God, the God of all creation, has chosen to use you for His purpose. I've also learned something else through Jeff's letter. It's God, not us, who determines the times and the occasions to spiritually impact the lives of His people. Regardless of what we think, regardless of the preparations we make to change others' lives, it's all determined by the will of God.

**I wanted to make an impression**

There's one thing I do remember about that FCA camp where God changed Jeff's life. I remember I was asked to give a testimony to all the campers participating in football. The night before, I stayed up until some ungodly hour in an attempt to come up with something really profound to say to all those football players. I wanted to make an impression; I wanted them to go home remembering what Reid Lamport said. I was looking for quotes, anecdotes, humorous stories, anything I could find that would leave an imprint on them and, oh, yes, I almost forgot, to glorify the Lord too. How foolish I was. To think I could concoct or manufacture something that could change someone's life was nothing short of spiritual arrogance. To no one's surprise, the testimony *I gave* was quite forgettable; you see the words were mine, not God's.

The talk with Jeff, on the other hand, took no preparation, yet the results were unfathomable. In Jeff's case, unlike the testimony to the football players, God provided the script, not I. It's been a little over two years since I received Jeff's letter, yet his words will be a source of encouragement to me for as long as I live. Almost twenty years ago I was prompted by the Lord to sit down and share His love and encouragement with a young man I barely knew; now that young man has returned to me that same love and encouragement a hundred-fold.

*Still other seed fell on good soil. It came up and yielded a crop, a*
*hundred times more than was sown.*
*(Luke 8:8)*

I can't even begin to tell you what receiving Jeff's letter has meant to me. The great thing about it is, each one of us have Jeffs we come in contact with every day. The question we have to be asking: Are we so busy searching for quotes, anecdotes and humorous stories that we're missing the opportunities God desires to simply speak through us?

*My message and my preaching were not with wise and persuasive words, but with a demonstration of the Spirit's power, so that your faith might not rest on men's wisdom but on God's power.*
*(1 Corinthians 2:4-5)*

### Remember...
- God is the ultimate source of all encouragement.
- No one else but God can change lives; to think we can is nothing short of spiritual arrogance.
- Quit searching for the perfect things to say and begin letting the voice of God speak through you.

### Is there a letter you should be sending?
Has someone inspired you who may not even be aware of it? Guess what; the only thing stopping them from knowing about it is you. It may not be as life-altering as Jeff's letter, but that's okay. The mere fact that you even remember them being an inspiration to you is reason enough for you to encourage them. Trust me, when they hear how God used them to inspire you, it will only serve to motivate them to look for new opportunities to inspire others.

## 24

# Selling the Product of Encouragement

*Then he said to them all: "If anyone would come after me, he must deny himself and take up his cross daily and follow me."*
*(Luke 9:23)*

The moment I began making notes and collecting data for this book, I have to admit I became a much better encourager. Not better as in my encouraging skills became quickly honed and eloquent, but better as in how much more conscious of encouraging I became. That's the first lesson to learn in becoming a person of encouragement. You must always be conscious of opportunities to encourage.

Once you become conscious of those opportunities, you'll be amazed at how often they appear. You'll actually wonder how it was possible to have missed them for so long. There's something else a true encourager does: He or she never waits for those opportunities to present themselves. A person committed to encourage looks for and finds his or her own opportunities.

It might help if we approach encouraging from the perspective of a salesperson. The idea that more contacts will obviously result in more sales is a philosophy taught in Business 101. Making your pitch to a hundred people will usually move more product than if you just show your wares to half that number. That same concept learned in business school holds true for those desiring to become successful encouragers. The more people you greet, the more people you engage in conversation, the more people you have the opportunity to encourage. (Hermits and recluses generally make very poor encouragers.) I hesitate in comparing general salespeople with encouragers for one particular reason: Salespeople do what they do to get rewarded with a paycheck, and while there is absolutely nothing wrong with making an honest living through sales, encouragers cannot be led by that same motivation.

> *Unlike so many, we do not peddle the word of God for profit.*
> *(2 Corinthians 2:17)*

## Life is about relationships

Jesus was, of course, the greatest salesman ever known. He sold Himself. Not a bad product to peddle; I wouldn't be surprised at all if it came with a lifetime guarantee. He turned no one away. He was constantly out and about, engaging people in conversation. And while He engaged them, He demonstrated a sincere interest in them as individuals. He wasn't a politician, shaking hands and kissing babies; He was their Savior, and His concern was for their soul. He was selling eternal life, and His success in doing so was often attributed to the encouraging way He spoke to others. At one point in His earthly ministry, He spoke the words:

> *Blessed are the poor in spirit, for theirs is*
> *the kingdom of heaven.*
> *(Matthew 5:3)*

I'll bet there were more than a few spiritually poor people listening to Him as He spoke those words of great encouragement. There were probably just as many being persecuted who heard these words:

> *Blessed are you when people insult you, persecute you and*
> *falsely say all kinds of evil against you because of me. Rejoice*
> *and be glad, because great is your reward in heaven, for the*
> *same way they persecuted the prophets who were before you.*
> *(Matthew 5:11)*

The Word of God teaches us that life is about relationships. Of utmost importance is our relationship to the Father through Christ. After that comes our relationship with one another by means of the Holy Spirit. When Jesus took the time to talk with people, that act alone became for them a sense of encouragement. Whether they were aware He was the Son of God or not, just knowing someone cared enough to spend time with them gave them the encouragement to go on.

As I became more conscious of encouraging, I began engaging myself and conversing more with others. The moment I began doing that, I started discovering something extremely important in the process. I found myself becoming genuinely concerned about who they were. It's not like I ignored them before or was unconcerned about their lives previously, but by consciously taking more time to talk with them, I learned more about who they were as people. I learned not only of issues they were struggling with that I could pray for, but also I began developing an understanding of why they are the way they are. And believe me, when you know some of the more personal issues in people's lives, it can go a long way in loving them as we're called to love them.

*My command is this: Love each other as I have loved you.*
*(John 15:12)*

Being a true encourager is really about selling the Christ in us. And we have to remember, selling Christ is much more akin to a privilege than it is a job. But like a job, it can sometimes get tedious. There are plenty of days I don't feel like talking to or even listening to other people; it might be that I'm tired, or quite frankly just not in the mood. But I also realize when my heart is intent on being an encourager, it's not about me.

If my goal is to encourage, and I am committed to my goal, then my selfish attitude has no option but to be put on hold. That's one of the great byproducts of being an encourager; there's no time for wallowing in selfishness because there's always someone around who could use a shoulder to lean on. While our privilege is to provide the shoulder, the desire and the power to do so belong to Christ. And even if they don't recognize that it's Christ in you who is listening to them and encouraging them, just knowing that someone cares enough to spend time with them can give them just the boost they need. I have come to learn that encouraging others is a lot like witnessing to them. As a matter of fact, I can say with a good deal of confidence, encouraging is a very effective form of witnessing.

*We sent Timothy, who is our brother and God's fellow worker in*
*spreading the gospel of Christ, to strengthen*
*and encourage you in your faith.*
*(1 Thessalonians 3:2)*

Jesus continues as a salesman today; only He has chosen you and me to go forth and sell His product. What we have to remember is, as He walked the earth offering freely His gift of eternal life, there were many who never bought into it. This tells us there are going to be people today who won't buy into it as well. However, Jesus never allowed any of the doors slammed in His face to discourage Him from knocking on the next one. And while there were many who chose not to receive His gift, He afforded everyone the opportunity.

We can learn a lot from Jesus' all-inclusive approach when it comes to witnessing through encouragement. Just as He didn't allow outward appearance or track records to hamper His effort of demonstrating his Father's love, neither should we. By approaching and encouraging only those whom we think will appreciate our encouragement, we're eliminating a significant number of people whose lives could benefit greatly from some of their Father's love. Don't allow other's initial reaction, or lack of reaction, to discourage you from exhorting and validating them. Unlike Jesus, we don't have the benefit of knowing what's going on in their hearts or their minds. Besides, our call is not to worry about such things; our call is to simply go forth and shine the light of God. Keep in mind, shining God's light successfully takes the same attributes it takes to be a successful salesman: commitment and perseverance.

*For this very reason, make every effort to add to your faith goodness; and to goodness, knowledge; and to knowledge, self-control; and to self-control, perseverance...For if you possess these qualities in increasing measure, they will keep you from being ineffective and unproductive.*
*(2 Peter 1:5-6,8)*

Perseverance is needed when we don't receive the kind of reaction we're looking for from others after speaking encouragement to them. A negative reaction should never be a deterrent to going on and pitching our product of encouragement to the next person. Something all successful salespeople possess is the common trait of never allowing their last encounter to adversely affect their next one. Their eyes are always looking forward as they persist relentlessly in an effort to win over the next person.

Now there's one other thing that separates the best from the rest when it comes to selling. It has to do with the product itself. People with a great product to sell know it, and that knowledge becomes for them a basis for confidence. Those who peddle something of value are convinced the lives of others will greatly benefit from what they have to offer. The confidence they possess from knowing people truly need what they have to sell translates to successful sales. Now let me ask you, what could possibly be of more value or benefit to anyone than receiving a generous portion of the love of Jesus? And another thing, those with a genuine product to sell never have to resort to tricks or gimmicks in an effort to get you to buy. Their product seems to pretty much sell itself.

Each one of us has the privilege every day of touting not only the most genuine product known to mankind, but also the most valuable. And here's the best part: We aren't paid on commission. As a matter-of-fact, there's not even a quota we have to meet. You see, our payment comes in the form of everlasting joy and contentment in knowing that the Creator of the Universe has employed us to be His conveyors of love through the privilege of encouraging others.

### *Remember...*
- Being a true encourager is really about selling the Christ in us.
- The more people you greet, the more people you engage in conversation, the more people you have the opportunity to encourage.
- Never allow your last encouraging encounter to adversely affect your next one.

### *Encouraging 101*
Okay, encouragers, you've just finished your coursework. Now it's time to take your final. Keep in mind any grade will be passing; you see, this course is graded on motive not outcome. Becoming a top student in Encouraging 101 has everything to do with making the effort and not in tangible results.

> *The Lord does not look at the things man looks at. Man looks*
> *at the outward appearance, but the Lord looks at the heart.*
> *(1 Samuel 16:7)*

Sort of takes the pressure off, doesn't it? There's no material to memorize, no data for you to concern yourself with and no charts or statistics to work into your presentation. You don't even have to concern yourself with what territory is yours. Yours is the entire world!

# 25

# "I'm So Proud of You"

*I have great confidence in you; I take great pride_in you.*
*I am greatly encouraged.*
*(2 Corinthians 7:4)*

I have recently learned that five of the most powerful words you can ever say to another human being are, "I'm so proud of you." Don't take my word for it; try it yourself. Nothing will light up the face of another person as much as those five words, and for good reason. There's remarkable validation in telling someone how proud you are of them, not proud of what they've done or what they've achieved, but proud of them as a person. People get commended for things they accomplish all the time. It's common place to applaud the achievements of people; we see it being done in every facet of life. But something we don't see all the time are standing ovations for people themselves. I know it might sound a little over-the-top, but I have learned there is nothing more valuable than people. I'm not saying there shouldn't be curtain calls or celebrations after outstanding performances; I'm just saying, what's wrong with putting your hands together for someone in the form of telling them how proud you are of them?

**Why can't you be proud of your mother-in-law?**

A dear friend of mine, Corny McKnight, has taught me many things about the Lord. His demeanor and his Christian walk are a source of inspiration and motivation for all who know him. His name on the other hand is reminiscent of some character on a Saturday morning children's show.

And while Corny has the personality that could easily entertain an audience of hyper-active kids for a half an hour, God has called him to enrich the lives of men. Corny has held countless men's Bible studies over the years, but it's the one-on-one impact he makes with other men that separates him from the typical teacher. If ever there was someone I knew who lived this next Scripture to a tee, it would be Corny.

> *Similarly, encourage the young men to be self-controlled. In everything set them an example by doing what is good. In your teaching show integrity, seriousness and soundness of speech that cannot be condemned, so that those who oppose you may be ashamed because they have nothing bad to say about us.*
> *(Titus 2:6-8)*

And while it's true, Corny has enhanced my life greatly by teaching me, among other things, integrity and sound speech, the most profound and impactful lesson I've learned from Corny came one day when he walked up to me in church and said, "Reid, I'm so proud of you." Rarely am I at a loss for words, but when he spoke those words, it took me completely by surprise, so much so, I wasn't sure how to respond. I knew Corny to be a man who wore his heart on his sleeve, but the intensity of those words coupled with the sincerity with which he spoke caught me at a loss. Not that I didn't appreciate it, because I surely did; it's just at fifty-six years of age, it wasn't something I was used to hearing. As a matter of fact, the only other people I can remember telling me they were proud of me was my mom and dad. I was fortunate to have parents who affirmed me as a child, and I can honestly say I never got tired of hearing them say how proud they were of me.

When Corny said it, however, there was something different, but in a good way. "I'm so proud of you" is not something one man expects to hear from another man. It's something parents or coaches or teachers say, and almost exclusively they say it to children, usually after they have done something out of the ordinary. Coming from adults to children, those words sound proper, appropriate. When an older generation speaks those words to a younger generation, no one bats an eye.

For some reason, though, it seems ill-suited when peers say it to one another. Why is that, I wonder. Why can't you be proud of, let's say, your best friend? Why can't you tell your brother, your wife, your parents or your mother-in-law just how proud you are of them? If we could be perfectly honest for a moment, I bet we'd find a lot of people in our lives that we are proud of but never tell. You want to know the reason we never tell them? We never tell them because it might make us appear different. Since telling another adult you're proud of them isn't common practice, we hesitate doing so in an effort to remain normal in the eyes of others. But where does it tell us in Scripture we are to live normally? I've read Scripture identifying us as a lot of things, but none of them identify us as normal. How about this one, for example?

*Dear friends, I urge you, as aliens and strangers in the world, to abstain from sinful desires, which war against your soul.*
*(1 Peter 2:11).*

Odd, peculiar, weird, unusual maybe, but as believers we should avoid being tabbed as normal, at all costs. I mean if we always come across as normal, how are people going to know there's something different about us? Normal to me is borrrrrring. Get a load of these synonyms for normal: usual, standard, regular, typical, ordinary, common, routine, average. If we lived our lives descriptive of these words, how would people ever get the impression that the God we serve is anything but ordinary? Here's the question we have to ask ourselves: Will telling someone we're proud of them be something Jesus would have done? That's all that matters. That's all that should ever matter. From everything I have read about Jesus in Scripture, the answer to that question is a resounding....YES! The apostle Paul saw enough merit in it to write it to an entire body of believers.

*I have great confidence in you; I take great pride in you.*
*I am greatly encouraged.*
*(2 Corinthians 7:4)*

I can't say how the Corinthians felt after reading those words from Pastor Paul, but I bet it didn't hurt their sense of self-worth any. Knowing there are others who are not only proud of us but also think enough about us to speak it out loud can do nothing but enhance our self-esteem. When Corny spoke those words to me for the first time, I may have been taken aback, but I can tell you this, I felt extremely validated. Now if we can validate one another and enhance each other's self-esteem merely by speaking five simple words, what could possibly hold us back? I've thought about this a lot, and trust me, there are no viable reasons for not telling someone you're proud of that you're proud of them, regardless of who they are.

**The last thing we want to appear is different**

Why is it we continue to be our own worst enemy? There should be only one rule when it comes to encouraging another human being, and that would be: There are no rules. If there's a reason at all to encourage someone else, and believe me we can always find a reason to encourage someone else, then by God we should go ahead and do it. The last thing on our minds should be to care what others might think. Time and again, we continue to stumble over our pride when it comes to expressing how we feel about other people. Every day we're presented with countless opportunities to validate someone else, but we hesitate in doing so because we don't want to be seen as different. When you begin to see it in that light, it should anger you. It angers me. To think of all the opportunities I've had over the years to inspire other people but chose not to because sharing my feelings might cause others to look at me in some weird way is, at the very least, embarrassing.

Corny has taught me something else as well. He subscribes to the theory that different is almost always better. What I mean by that is, he doesn't care if his actions, his words or his enthusiasm draw strange looks; he is committed to encouraging people, not pleasing people. What a difference in those two actions. Seems to me there's a Scripture verse covering that very philosophy:

> *Am I now trying to win the approval of men, or*
> *of God? Or am I trying to please men?*
> *If I were trying to please men, I would not be*
> *a servant of Christ.*
> *(Galatians 1:10)*

The truth is, to be a true servant of the Lord means there are times we're going to have to stand out from the crowd. Let me rephrase that. As true servants of the Lord, there are going to be very few times in our lives where we're not supposed to stand out from the crowd. Whether we're standing out because of something we're doing that others are admiring us for, or we're standing out because others think we've completely lost our minds, it shouldn't matter. Too often, Christ followers gauge what they should do, not by the Word of God, but by the reaction of people. The truth of the matter is, we ought to be getting strange looks everywhere we go; and if we're not, then we're probably not doing what God has called us to do, or we're probably not being what God has called us to be.

The trait of being different is probably the most difficult attribute of Christ His followers are asked to reveal. After all, it goes against every ounce of our flesh. Our flesh wants to be admired, and our flesh wants to be popular. The one thing the flesh doesn't want to do is appear different. There is nothing in our physical makeup that desires to go against the flow of popular opinion. Those who have chosen to do so have made the hard-line decision not to listen to what their flesh is telling them. Instead they are listening to the Spirit.

*Those who live in accordance with the Spirit have their minds set on what the Spirit desires. (Romans 8:5)*

It's true, the last thing most of us want is to appear different. However, when we read Scriptures such as Ephesians 5:1 and realize our only obligation is to imitate the Lord, we find ourselves in a dilemma. Should we listen to our flesh telling us how embarrassed it is to be seen as weird, or listen to and obey the Word of God regardless of how it puts our lives on display? Sometimes we try to represent the Lord while also attempting to keep our differences on the Q-T. Talk about an exercise in futility. It's as if someone says to me, "Hey, Reid, I want you to demonstrate the nature of Jesus Christ as you teach, coach and otherwise live your life; only try your best to see that nobody notices."

How ridiculous is that? As a follower of the Word, not only are we going to naturally stand out, but we're expected to stand out. That's not the philosophy of the world, which tells us to hide anything that's going to make people notice there's something different about us, especially when that difference has a chance of being controversial. You see the dilemma? As a believer, it doesn't take long before we discover how virtually impossible it is to represent our Lord and still blend in. It's God's desire for us to share His love and His Word with those we meet. When we do, the world tells us, "Just be prepared to get ridiculed." That's certainly how the world treated Jesus.

*Then the whole assembly rose and led him (Jesus) off...*
*The chief priests and the teachers of the law were standing*
*there, vehemently accusing him. Then Herod and his soldiers*
*ridiculed and mocked him.*
*(Luke 23:1,10-11)*

It's true, living our lives just like everyone else and saying only the things others expect us to say will probably save us from being ridiculed and mocked, but also it will keep others from seeing and hearing the Christ who is in us. The last thing we should be doing is listening to a world that tells us in no uncertain terms:

- "Don't reveal your feelings to someone else; you might stand out in a crowd."
- "Don't let down your guard; others might sense that as weakness."
- "Keep your distance, and you'll never have to get involved."
- "Play the game and others will accept you."
- "Whatever you do, don't tell someone else you're proud of them. That's just stupid; who do you think you are, their dad?"

When it comes down to it, the only reason we don't tell others we're proud of them is because we choose not to. It's difficult to imagine how many lives we could invigorate, how many attitudes we could stimulate and how many people we could motivate by simply telling others how proud we are of them. My guess is countless.

"I'm so proud of you." Sounds pretty simple, huh? That's because it is; the only thing making it difficult is us. If you're not sure you can step right up and start telling those around you that you're proud of them, my suggestion is to ease into it by telling your children or someone else's children you're proud of them. Chances are they're not hearing it enough anyway. Whatever you do, don't wait for some exceptional event or extraordinary action before telling someone how proud you are of them. The one thing that practice does, especially to our children, is reinforce to them that we're only proud of them when they do something special. Tell your son or daughter that you're proud of them today and that your pride is a result of them being who they are, not because of what they do. (Just make sure it's not right after Junior shaved the cat.) The more you begin speaking those words to your children, the easier it will become to tell your spouse the same thing. From there it's but a short step to using that same phrase with your friends and others in your life.

I recently began telling my students how proud I am of them. I'm embarrassed to admit that I've been teaching for thirty-seven years and just lately started using that phrase. I've encouraged them in the past, I've complimented them often, but I have to tell you, their reaction is not the same. Their demeanor is different after hearing their teacher say, "I'm so proud of you." It's true, they seem to light up, and they also seem to put forth more effort as a result. It's almost as though they're willing to do anything to hear those words again.

I have spent years studying behavior management. I've attempted literally hundreds of different reinforcement techniques in an effort to motivate my students. Little did I know that the most effective technique could be implemented by simply telling them, "I'm so proud of you." Let's take a look at what it is about these words that make them so powerful.

**It's powerful because it empowers others**

When you tell someone you're proud of them, in reality you're saying (according to Mr. Webster) that you are "drawing delight or elation" from your relationship with them. By saying, "I'm so proud of you," you are letting the person know that you are benefiting in some way from their life. This signifies to them, they have worth. To know that our life is in some way enhancing someone else's life validates us. It informs us that we are making a difference; and who doesn't want to think they are making a difference in the lives of other people? It's a powerful phrase. It's powerful because it empowers others.

When you speak the phrase "I'm so proud of you," you're supplying the person with knowledge, knowledge that they would otherwise not possess. When a person is made aware of their benefit to your life, they immediately see themselves in a brand new light, and that new light has value. Knowing that our lives have value enables us to live more confidently, more securely and ultimately more joyfully. By merely validating someone else through phrases like "I'm so proud of you," we are able to enrich their life with virtually little or no effort at all. The most difficult part is allowing the words to go forth; but just like anything else we're not used to doing, it only takes that first time to find out how easy it was all along. My prayer is that you begin today. The results will be immediate and they will be impactful. The thing that will surprise you the most will be how simple it is.

Corny has not only opened a gigantic door for me, but also he has encouraged me to go boldly through it. It is the "I don't care what anyone thinks as long as God gets the glory" door. I've been pretty tentative in stepping through it in the past. Praise the Lord, I have people in my life who constantly remind me there are a lot more important things than worrying about how others see me. I want to end this chapter by quoting a Scripture that further describes my friend to all of you. This one is rather accurate:

> *Cornelius... and all his family were devout and God-fearing.*
> *(Acts 10:1-2)*

I have no way of knowing if Cornelius' centurion friends called him Corny, but I have to admit this Scripture accurately portrays my friend's life to a tee. In all my life, I have yet to meet a more God-fearing or more devout family than Corny's.

*Author's note:* My friend Corny has recently been diagnosed with pancreatic cancer. He's facing a tough battle, however, he and his wife, Dolly, have been overwhelmed by the amount of encouragement they've been receiving. Almost everyone they know (and many they don't know) are calling, sending cards, praying and offering words of support. And while Corny and his wife have been overwhelmed by the love shown to them by so many, it comes as no surprise to all who know him. You see, God has a way of blessing those who spend their lives investing in the lives of others.

***Remember...***
- To be a true servant of the Lord, there are going to be very few instances where we're not supposed to stand out from the crowd.
- There's remarkable validation in telling someone how proud you are of them.
- Knowing there are others who are not only proud of us but also think enough about us to speak it can do nothing but enhance our self-esteem.

***It's your turn***
I can't wait for you to try this out! There's no doubt about it, it's going to take boldness and it's going to take the risk of being different. But let me tell you, the rewards far outweigh the risks. So where are you going to start? With your kids? Your spouse? If you ask me, you can't go wrong with either one of those starting points. Hey, you can't go wrong with any starting point. Who doesn't need to hear how proud someone is of them? I want you to make an effort to write and let me know just how impactful those five words have become in your life. Share with me how others reacted when you told them how proud you were of them. I'm willing to bet the majority of the blessing will remain on you!

E-mail me at: rlamport@unleashingthepowerofencouragement.com.

*Update on the author's note:* Corny graduated from this life a few months after the completion of this book. His impact on other's lives will undoubtedly remain timeless. He leaves behind a legacy of impacted people. People who were fortunate enough to hear, first-hand, just how proud he was of them, people who I believe will carry his torch of risking the odd looks and raised eyebrows from those in the world in an effort to shine the light of Jesus in their lives.

"Jesus, will you tell my friend just how proud I am of him"!

## Part 5

# Results from Encouraging

*While true encouragers don't set out with the goal of receiving, the benefits found from enhancing the lives of others are many.*

# 26

# The Reward of Encouraging

*What is due me is in the Lord's hand, and my*
*reward is with my God.*
*(Isaiah 49:4)*

If you're looking to get rewarded in some way by being an encourager to other people, you're going to get let down. That's not to say encouraging other people isn't rewarding, because nothing could be farther from the truth. However, if your motive for encouraging others is to earn brownie points with God or someone else, you're better off keeping your encouragement to yourself.

God calls us to encourage others for their sake, not ours. The philosophy behind *doing something to get something* is motivated out of greed. When your motivation is greed, you're no longer doing what you're doing out of love and obedience; you're doing it out of selfishness. Let me tell you, there's nothing ambiguous about God's feelings toward greed and selfishness.

*For of this you can be sure: No immoral, impure or greedy*
*person... has any inheritance in the kingdom*
*of Christ and of God.*
*(Ephesians 5:5)*

Encouragement, as God defines it, comes from a motivation of love and obedience. When you encourage others with a sincere heart, you're putting love into action. You're not only enacting a love for those you're

181

encouraging, but also you're demonstrating a love for God through your obedience. You'll find there will be times when you need no motivation whatsoever to encourage someone; it'll seem as though it just flows out of you, as if it was the purpose for which you were created. But because we're human, which means our feelings are never the same from one moment to the next, there will also be times when the last thing you feel like doing is speaking encouragement to someone else.

The need to encourage someone might come at a time when you your-self are feeling a little tired of always being the encourager; as if it might kill someone else to throw a little encouragement your way every now and again. It's easy to get into the mindset of self-centeredness, which is based on feelings, and it's solely responsible for the vast majority of our encouragement never making it to the ears of those who need it most. When we start making life solely about us, we need to recognize what we're doing and take authority over it immediately. If we don't and we allow our self-ishness the right to be heard, it will almost always seize control of our thoughts and sabotage our desire to live obediently unto God. If you ever find this happening (I should say *when* you find this happening), you need to press in and follow God's call and not your own self-centered feelings.

> *Do nothing out of selfish ambition.*
> *(Philippians 2:3)*

Listening to our feelings will usually lead us away from God's call and rarely to it. True obedience is listening to and then obeying our Master, regardless of how we're feeling. Encouraging others is God's call for every one of us, and often it takes the form of sacrifice unto the Lord, not sacrifice so much as in doing something we don't want to do, but sacrifice as in replacing what we want in lieu of what God wants. No one knew better the heart of God than David; that's why he wrote:

> *I desire to do your will O my God.*
> *(Psalm 40:8)*

Our spirit person desires to do God's will; it's this body of flesh that wants to live contrary to God's desires. When we learn to listen to God's call and proceed to carry it out, regardless of what we feel like doing or not, it is seen as a sacrifice unto the Lord. A sacrifice that is acceptable before our Lord, I might add. Our sacrifices are only acceptable when brought to God with an attitude of love and loyalty. When we attempt to encourage others from any other attitude, it is false encouragement. This includes the incentive to encourage others in an effort to be rewarded somewhere down the line. We're treading on dangerous ground whenever we attempt to earn something from the Lord for our righteous acts. The Pharisees earned Jesus' wrath by doing holy and righteous acts to secure favor with God.

> *Woe to you teachers of the law and Pharisees, you hypocrites!*
> *You are like whitewashed tombs, which look beautiful on the*
> *outside but on the inside are full of dead men's bones and*
> *everything unclean.*
> *(Matthew 23:27)*

The point Jesus so emphatically made time and time again was that anything we do for the Lord must be done with no personal incentive. Too often things are done that look impressive and holy, but the motive by which they're done is selfish and greedy. If we merely go through the motion of encouraging someone because it looks good and it helps to fill up our *good deeds basket*, then what applied to the Pharisees also applies to us. The result will then be "woe to us."

> *You know we never used flattery nor did we*
> *put on a mask to cover up greed.*
> *( 1 Thessalonians 2:5)*

It's important to understand that no amount of living holy, no amount of doing good and no amount of encouraging others will make us even one ounce more righteous. Christ earned us all the righteousness we're ever going to need as well as all the righteousness we're ever going to get; He did so the moment He went to the cross. If we could earn our own righteousness by good works and encouraging others, then that cross is made void of any power whatsoever.

**If it's done in selfishness, it can't be love**

When speaking encouragement with selfish motives, the words we use may seem good and accurate, but the motivation behind them is flawed. Blessings will not result from anything done with flawed motives. If I compliment you with the intent that you're going to compliment me in return, I haven't demonstrated one ounce of God's love.

*And if you lend to those from whom you expect*
*repayment, what credit is that to you?*
*Even 'sinners' lend to 'sinners', expecting*
*to be repaid in full.*
*(Luke 6:34)*

The power behind encouraging rests in the motive of the encourager. If my motive is to validate you and inspire you, God will carry forth those words and accomplish their purpose. If my motive has a selfish purpose, that too will be brought to light. Obedience is what God is after. In other words, it only matters to God *why* we do what we do. God isn't as concerned so much with what we do as He is with our reason for doing it. We're reminded of that in the Book of Hebrews:

*For the word of God…judges the thoughts*
*and attitudes of the heart.*
*(Hebrews 4:12)*

It's God's intention that His children become conformed to the likeness of His Son. Since Christ's motives are pure, ours should be pure as well. We can hide our motives from one another, but keeping them from God is impossible.

*Nothing in all creation is hidden from God's sight. Everything is*
*uncovered and laid bare before the eyes*
*of Him to whom we must give account.*
*(Hebrews 4:13)*

So you see when we do seemingly good things, even things in the church, but we're doing them to get recognized or rewarded, God will not bless them. There is only one reason for us to do anything for the Lord. We must do what we do out of obedience because obedience is a demonstration of our love. Jesus said:

*If you love me, you will obey what I command.*
*(John 14:15)*

Do you love God? Yes? Then obey Him. When He tells us to love one another, it's imperative we take Him at His word.

*Love... is not self-seeking.*
*(1 Corinthians 13:5)*

By virtue of this Scripture, we see that anything done with a selfish motive can't be love, even though it may look like love. We are to examine ourselves, our thoughts, our purposes, looking for anything fitting the description of self-seeking. And when we find it (believe me, it will be there), we are to repent and ask God to remove it and in its place fill us with more of Him. Is being an encourager rewarding? Amazingly rewarding! Knowing that our sincere encouragement will bless the heart of God, as well as the heart of man, is incredibly rewarding. To know we're making a difference in someone else's life, as we live out God's purpose for our life, is as satisfying as it gets. We just have to keep in mind, rewards aren't always immediate.

*Wait till the Lord comes. He will bring to light what is hidden*
*in darkness and will expose the motives of men's hearts. At that*
*time each will receive his praise from God.*
*(1 Corinthians 4:5)*

**It not only feels good, it's good for us**
Encouragement carries with it the unique quality of pleasing both our flesh and the Spirit. Good luck finding many things that do that! Scripture tells us that our sinful nature (flesh) is in opposition to that which pleases God (Spirit). What pleases our sinful nature does not satisfy the Spirit of God who lives in us. By that same token, what pleases God is usually, at best, unpleasant to the flesh. For example, take discipline:

*The Lord disciplines those he loves.*
*(Proverbs 3:12)*

Discipline is beneficial; otherwise God would not apply it to those He loves. And while it may be beneficial, our flesh doesn't want anything to do with it. Our flesh has its own agenda, and chances are there's nothing on that agenda that refers to discipline. Discipline rarely feels good, and since the flesh has only one interest in mind, and that is the interest of feeling good, discipline has to be something the flesh is made to experience. For example, have you ever caught yourself driving to the gym to work out and all of a sudden think, "Where am I going," only to realize your body has taken your mind captive to go work out? Ridiculous, huh? But I bet there are plenty of times when your mind has to do all it can to convince and even plead with your body, "Come on, it's time to go work out."

Look at unforgiveness. We know unforgiveness is a sin and displeases our Father. The only reason we harbor unforgiveness is because it gives our flesh so much pleasure; otherwise, knowing what God thinks of it, we'd drop it like a bad habit. Unforgiveness gives us a false sense of control over whomever it is we're holding bitterness. We like that control, at least our flesh does. So we see that unforgiveness, although it grieves the Spirit, pleases our flesh. Just think how difficult it is to forgive someone who doesn't deserve to be forgiven. Forget difficult; *impossible* is more like it. Without the power of God at work in our lives, we will find it virtually impossible to forgive people we deem as unworthy to be forgiven. Our flesh has to be made to submit (be disciplined) in order for us to experience the freedom God's forgiveness brings to those who forgive.

What makes encouragement so special is knowing that it not only feels good, but also it's good for us. It satisfies the whole person, Spirit and flesh. That's how you know it's from God. It's also why you never have to stop and pray about whether or not you should encourage someone; it's one of the easiest decisions you'll ever have to make. If you see someone you admire for the way they live their life, tell them. If someone possesses a quality you respect, let them know. You don't have to have a reason to encourage someone; you just have to have a desire to touch their heart.

**Potential encouragement has no benefit**

We should be doling out encouragement left and right, giving it away at every opportunity. Encouraging others should be a ceaseless and continuous action we adopt as a regular part of our day. It should flow through us without us even having to think about it. Unfortunately, we're more inclined to treat it as though it were an Oscar-winning performance. "Ladies and gentlemen, in the category of 'Encouraging Male Persons,' this next gentleman has esteemed his children and affirmed those around him to the point that all who know him feel confident and appreciated..."

I don't think so. Encouraging should be seen as something natural, something typical, not some award-winning action. And parents should be especially conscious of practicing it. When your children leave the house, bless them. Tell them you're proud of them and that you're glad they belong to you. Esteem them when they go out and when they come in. You don't have to do it with bells and whistles as though it's some kind of rehearsed production. Just seize the opportunity and speak validation into them. It's an investment that will one day pay remarkable dividends.

Understand, encouraging in general never has to be made into a major production, which tends to shine too much light on the encourager, and that's not why we're doing it. Encouragement is best served when it comes during normal conversation or when written in an intimate note. The more personal you make it, the more enthusiastically it will be received. There are times when encouraging others in the presence of others is quite appropriate; and there are times when maybe it's not. Either way, you'll get your opportunity. Just make sure you take it.

Potential encouragement has no benefit whatsoever; it has to be released. Make it a habit of releasing yours regularly. And as you do so with no ulterior motivation attached, just be prepared to handle the onslaught of personal blessings when they come, blessings that are destined to last for quite a while!

*Behold, I am coming soon! My reward is with me.*
*(Revelation 22:12)*

### Remember...
- When you encourage others with a sincere heart, you're putting God's love into action.
- Encouragement is unique in that it not only feels good, but it's also good for us.
- Encouraging never has to be made into a major production, which tends to shine too much light on the encourager.
- If your motivation for encouraging is to get recognized or rewarded in some way, you're going to get let down. God will not bless actions done in an attempt to serve ourselves.

### Make it about others
Encouraging is truly our "two birds with one stone" scenario. It takes the focus off of us and at the same time it accentuates the lives of others. This philosophy bodes well with just about everything Jesus taught regarding how we're to love one another. While it may take a little time convincing our flesh that encouraging is something we need to do, our flesh will quickly come to appreciate how it feels as our words of encouragement reach the ears and hearts of others.

# 27

# Victory Through the Encouragement of God's Word

*But thanks be to God! He gives us the victory*
*through our Lord Jesus Christ.*
*(1 Corinthians 15:57)*

I don't care who you are; you like to win. Obviously winning is more important to some than it is to others. But in fifty-nine years, I have yet to meet anyone who would opt to lose if given a choice. For believers, winning in this life is directly proportional to one thing, our obedience to the word of God. It's God's desire that His people prosper; we know this from reading His History Book and seeing that when God's people listened and heeded His word, they prospered. However, when those same people began living disobediently by compromising and altering His word, poverty was the result. Now keep in mind that the prosperity and poverty I speak about here has nothing to do with portfolios or bank accounts, but it has everything to do with triumphal living, because triumphal living is exactly how God desires us to exist.

*But thanks be to God, who always leads us in*
*triumphal procession in Christ.*
*(2 Corinthians 2:14)*

If we take these two Scripture verses from Paul's letters to the Corinthians at face value, we see that God "gives us victory" and "leads us in triumphal procession." Triumph and victory, that's pretty exciting stuff! Who doesn't want to lay their head on their pillow at night knowing they had a day marked by winning? And as you read and meditate on these Scriptures I want you to notice there are no strings attached, no words of contingency. The apostle Paul doesn't say, "God will give us the victory" and "God will lead us in triumphal procession **if** ..." No, the Word simply says, God *gives* and God *leads*. The only two requirements needed to experience the promises of these verses are to *receive* and to *follow*. That's what God desires for all of His children. That shouldn't be too difficult, should it? Receive from God and follow Him, and His promise is to lead us into victory. Now before we begin planning the celebration party, I am led to inform you (as if you weren't already aware), it's not as easy as it may seem. There's one thing that continually interferes with following God's word once we've received it. I believe it was Walter Crawford Kelly who said it best: "We have met the enemy and he is us."

More than anything else, it's our own flesh that will sabotage our obedience in receiving and following God. Our flesh person has the uncanny ability to convince our spirit person that it knows better than the Word of God what's best for us. I don't know about you, but my flesh has made way too many decisions without consulting me first. When permitted to do so, our flesh will invariably live by the mantra of the world: "If it feels good, do it." The problem with living by that philosophy is there is nothing in our flesh that feels even the slightest bit of loyalty to God.

Victorious living, as Christ has provided it for us, entails us following Him, not the world. It's incredible to think that thousands of years have passed and nothing has changed, at least nothing of eternal value. God is still God; we are still His people; and His Word remains timeless.

*Heaven and earth will pass away, but my words*
*will never pass away.*
*(Matthew 24:35)*

What I find to be astonishing is our continual desire to alter the words of God; as if God needs our help in composing His commands to us. Far too often we take the words given to us by the Creator of the Universe and put them through personal rewrite after rewrite in an effort to fit them to our lives. The Word of God was never designed to fit around our lives. Our lives, however, were created to be lived according to His Word.

You'd think, given the fact that many of us are semi-intelligent people, that the truth of that statement would eventually sink in and we'd just come to accept it as a way of life. You would also think that after centuries of reading about the devastation experienced in the lives of those who throughout history altered the Word of God, mankind would have wised up a bit.

Obviously we've got a ways to go. Changing God's Word didn't work hundreds or thousands of years ago and neither does it work today. Here's the way it does work; God establishes His Word, gives it to us for our benefit, and we either accept it as is or reject it. There's no such thing as editing the Word of God. A prime example is the concept of faith.

*We live by faith and not by sight.*
*(2 Corinthians 5:7)*

It's a perfect plan as long as we follow it. But in our eyes it makes more sense to trust in what we see and what we know; so we reconfigure what God says by attaching conditions to it. Now it reads something like: "We live by faith and not by sight (until we run into something we can handle better on our own)."

We may not come right out and say that because of how incredibly foolish it sounds, but based upon the number of times we've chosen to ignore God's word in order to follow our own speaks differently. And how many times after following our own instincts in lieu of following Him have we come out on top? (That's a rhetorical question.) Coming out on top or experiencing victory in our lives, true victory not temporary success, is directly proportional to our obedience in living faithfully by God's decrees.

**Anxiety is worrying about what may or may not be**

Living obediently to God's Word is the manifestation of faith (total dependence on God). It's also a full-time way of life and not a part-time action. God gave us faith so that regardless of our circumstances, our dependence on Him wouldn't need to change. In spite of what we may think, we need God just as much when life is rolling along carefree as we do when the bottom is about to drop out. God's desire is for us to live in daily reliance upon Him, no matter what the day may bring. God wants us so used to Him being in charge that nothing we face will ever develop into anxiety and fear, because anxiety and fear, as most of us are aware, are tied a whole lot closer to defeat than they are to victory.

*Cast all your anxiety on him because he cares for you.*
*(1 Peter 5:7)*

When Peter tells us to cast our anxiety, he means just that. We are to take all circumstances that produce anxiety in our lives and direct them toward our Father. Casting our anxieties doesn't mean we stop attempting to improve our circumstances by lying back and letting God handle everything. It does mean, however, we're not going to allow the results of our circumstances, or what could be the results of our circumstances, to consume us. Anxiety comes as a result of us worrying over what may or may not be, even though what may or may not be is completely out of our control. When the things of this life and their impending outcomes begin to overwhelm us, you can assuredly bet it's a result of us taking our eyes off Jesus. Peter took his eyes off Jesus for a split second and nearly drowned!

*But when he saw the wind, he was afraid and, (began) to sink.*
*(Matthew 14:30)*

Too often, just like Peter, we find ourselves up to our neck in water, troubled over circumstances that are out of our control. When that happens, we need to go back and see how Peter recovered from his near-death experience. Scripture tells us he cried out:

*Lord, save me! (Matthew 14:30)*

and of course Jesus did.

Now if you're at all like me, calling out to Jesus for help is something I often find myself doing; it's just unfortunate that the majority of the time my cry for help follows a sequence of unsuccessful attempts to dogpaddle myself to shore. For some reason, I too often turn to the Lord only after my self-help remedies have been exhausted. You'd have thought I would have learned my lesson by now, wouldn't you, seeing as how I'm a pastor and all. Maybe it was all the hits I took on the head playing college football. Yeah, that must be it; Lord knows it doesn't have anything to do with the amount of pride still hanging around. Excuse me for a second, "Lord, please forgive me for the blatant lie I just wrote and help me in my ongoing struggle towards humility. Amen." Thought it best not to wait until the end of the chapter.

Okay, where was I? Oh, yeah, attempting to pull ourselves out of dilemma after dilemma instead of crying out to the Lord first will invariably waste not only time and energy, it will also usher in a great deal of stress in the process. And stress, as we have been told time and again by the medical profession, is the number one cause of heart disease. Why is it we humans put ourselves through such unnecessary self-inflicting measures? Seriously, rarely will we miss an opportunity to wring our hands in worry today over tomorrow's dilemmas. We'll stand in church and sing, "Trust and Obey," but before we close the hymnal our blood pressure is up twenty points, agonizing over a problem we may have to face at work on Monday. That's not focusing our eyes on Christ. Focusing our eyes on Christ will have but two results, and neither one has anything to do with worry. Actually they're antidotes for worry. Those results I've come to discover the hard way are *peace* and *security*. God knows all this far better than we do; I'm convinced it's why He prompted the Psalmist to write:

> *Blessed is the man...who finds great delight in (God's)*
> *commands. His heart is **secure**, he will have no fear;*
> *in the end he will look in triumph on his foes.*
> *(Psalm 112:1,8*, emphasis mine*)*

When our hearts are secure, there's an absence of worry, and when our hearts are at peace, there's a... well, here, it will be much more profound coming from King Solomon:

> *A heart at **peace** gives life to the body.*
> *(Proverbs 14: 30*, emphasis mine)

Security, an absence of fear, life to our bodies, triumph, and blessedness. These are the results of us focusing our eyes on Jesus. Now compare those to the lead-balloon result achieved by Peter the moment he took his eyes off Jesus. Not even close, is it?

### Faith doesn't flee

Do you remember Jesus' rebuke to Peter as He raised him up from the water? Let me refresh your memory. He said:

> *You of little faith, why did you doubt?*
> *(Matthew 14:31)*

I'm convinced Jesus wasn't rebuking Peter for not possessing enough faith; I believe Jesus was rebuking Peter for not enacting the faith he possessed. Contrary to what some may believe, faith doesn't need to be mustered up; faith needs only to be relied upon. One thing I've discovered that can help jump-start the faith we already possess is encouragement. Regardless of what we may feel, our faith hasn't abandoned us. Faith doesn't flee. It's not here one moment and gone the next. It can seem that way when things such as worry, fear and anxiety have crept into our daily lives. What we have to remember is that fear, worry and the like are emotions, a state of mind. They're not the realities of our spiritual life in Christ.

*There is no fear in love. But perfect love drives out fear.*
*(1 John 4:18)*

No one could love us more than our perfect God. Do you really think He would allow fear to trump His faith? (Rhetorical question number two.) Since it's God who gives us faith, His portion to us would certainly be one of adequacy.

*The apostles said to the Lord, "Increase our faith!"*
*(Luke 17:5)*

If you don't recall Jesus' response to His disciples' desire for more faith, it was based in His teaching on what just a little faith can do.

*He replied, "If you have faith as small as a mustard seed,*
*you can say to this mulberry tree, be uprooted and planted*
*into the sea, and it will obey you."*
*(Luke 17:6)*

You see, more faith isn't necessary. But often what is necessary is someone reminding us of the faith we already possess, just as Jesus did in this portion of Scripture to His disciples. And, yes, it would be nice if we had the Lord Himself walking around teaching us of mustard seeds and pointing out mulberry trees, but since at the moment He's in heaven sitting at the right hand of the Father, we'll have to rely upon one another to do so. As children of light and possessors of God's Spirit, we are responsible for assuming the role of "Christ the Encourager" and speaking forth those inspiring words of Jesus. We have been entrusted with reminding one another that God has indeed provided each of us with sufficient faith to live triumphantly. That's the beauty of possessing the Holy Spirit of God; we are enabled to demonstrate Jesus to the world.

*I tell you the truth, anyone who has faith in me will do
what I have been doing.
He will even do greater things than these, because
I am going to the Father.
(John 14:12)*

One of the things Jesus did perfectly was to encourage. I have heard a number of teachings on this John 14 Scripture, and the vast majority of them deal with our ability to perform the miracles of Jesus through the power of the Holy Spirit. And while I don't in any way refute those teachings, I will suggest rather emphatically that it can also refer to our ability to be the encourager Jesus was and is. After all, we possess His Spirit, the very being responsible for carrying out all the encouraging Christ has ever given; it only makes sense that we too are capable of the same encouraging.

This incident on Galilee wasn't the only time Peter chose to rely on his sight rather than Jesus' command. He suffered through a number of "learning it the hard way" lessons before he eventually got it right. And just like Peter, it can take us a number of years attending the spiritual school of hard knocks before we get it right. It would be nice if enacting faith came as second nature to us, but the reality of life tells us differently. I will say, however, that the more we trust God, the more we step out in faith, the easier it becomes the next time Jesus calls for us to come out of the boat.

The truth is, faithful living *is* victorious living, and only those who possess the Spirit of God can experience it. Faith comes initially to us not as a result of acting righteous, but as a result of our "righteous standing" before God. It's really a by-product of our relationship with Christ. However, it only works when we go out and enact it in our lives. Crying out to the Lord after we've exhausted all other avenues is not living by faith; it's more like living by the process of elimination. But how often do you find yourself guilty of possessing the following attitude? "Let's see, since all my efforts didn't work, I suppose the only thing left is to give God a try."

### God's track record is flawless

Living by faith is learning to go to the Father *first*; and in choosing to go that route we are spared a good number of headaches. There is one thing we must learn to do, though, once we place our lives in the hands of our Father. We are no longer to worry about the outcome. Let's go back to Peter stepping out of the boat. Peter asked for assurance that the image he saw was indeed Jesus.

*Lord, if it's you, tell me to come to you on the water.*
*(Matthew 14:28)*

Jesus confirmed it by telling Peter to "come." We all know that Peter went. The story would have had a much different ending had Peter continued to walk in faith instead of worrying about the outcome. The moment Peter's faith enabled him to place his life in the hands of Jesus and step over the side of that boat, he experienced the supernatural. What I so often fail to grasp when reading this account in Scripture is that this mortal fisherman was, at one point, successfully walking on top of the Sea of Galilee!

The majority of the teachings I've read on this Scripture tend to focus on Peter's lack of faith and the failure that resulted. Why can't we look at it from a little different angle and see the amazing victory Peter's employment of faith produced? Come on now; is that glass half full or isn't it? We see at the onset of this phenomenon Peter casting his worries on the Master. No one could ever argue that Peter hadn't, at least initially, trusted in Jesus' ability to handle the situation. From the get-go Peter chose to turn over his fears to Christ, and the moment he did, the result was one of victory. His downfall (no pun intended) came when he attempted to take back those fears and deal with them on his own. Had Peter remained trustful of Jesus' ability to master the laws of the universe, there's no telling what could have resulted. One lesson we can take away from Peter's encounter on the water with Jesus is this: Once we've given Him our worries and anxieties, don't attempt to take them back!

Our family is at this moment preparing to leave for vacation. And when it comes to the planning of such events you could say my wife, Michele, is a worrier. Wait, that doesn't sound very nice, does it? Okay, how about if I suggest that the preparation for vacation tends to make her a bit anxiety-ridden? Gee, that's not a whole lot better. Hmm, alright, let's just say she is a meticulously exhaustive planner to the nth degree. I, on the other hand, plan about as unmeticulously and inexhaustively as possible, which tends to add considerably to Michele's inclination to obsessively pack for vacation as though she were Dustin Hoffman in *Rainman*. (Good Lord, where is this headed?)

Now, every year she gives me certain responsibilities for the trip, like loading up the car and making sure I've packed enough socks, underwear and toiletries. She says it's not that she doesn't trust me with the really important stuff; it's just that she knows what needs to go and what doesn't. (I don't buy that for a moment.)

Every year she tells me, "Honey, I'm not going to worry about your stuff or the stuff for the car or the beach because you've got it covered, right?"

"That's right, I've got it covered."

If it ended there, you and I wouldn't be having this conversation. I also wouldn't have a story to drive home my point of letting things go. Anyway, as you might have guessed, as the time for departure draws near, Michele begins going through a series of checks and double-checks to make sure I've truly taken care of "my stuff."

"Honey, we don't know what the weather is going to be for the entire week. You know how weathermen are. Did you pack a sweatshirt?"

"Got it."

"Now make sure you pack all six beach chairs just in case everyone wants to sit down at the same time."

"Check."

"You'll have to pack your own sun tan lotion; I'm only packing mine."

"It's in my travel bag as we speak."

"Did you remember to check the pressure in the tires? 'Cause last year we got a flat tire and I don't want to get another one."

"Took care of it this morning."

It feels so good to know I'm able to lighten Michele's burden over worrying about vacation!

Now I must confess, my reputation for "forgetting" to pack a number of necessary items the past twenty years gives her more than ample reason to be concerned. No such concern, however, should ever cross our mind when it comes to giving God our worries. But too often that's exactly what our attitude is saying.

"Here, God, I'm giving You the stress of worrying about my children. You deal with the anxiety and the angst of being their parent, because as of now I'm casting it on You just like Your Word says."

Now that sounds good and all, but within a short amount of time we find ourselves checking back with God to make sure He's properly handling His responsibility.

"Hey, God, You know what? I think it would be a good idea if You would convict my daughter into going to church on Sunday. Maybe by being there she will begin to see the love......"

"Excuse me, Father, I just wanted to remind You that my son tends to hang out with some shady characters, so I was thinking if You could just steer them away from him and have him meet some nice Christian friends, then......"

And while my wife may have good reason to question my ability to handle the responsibility of getting everything in the car for vacation, when it comes to us questioning God's ability to handle what we've given over to Him, we don't have a leg to stand on. You see, His track record for handling such things is flawless.

Worry and stress result from our lack of enacting the faith we've been given, and they are deterrents to living victoriously in this life. Gifts from God such as faith and encouragement are allies to victorious living; they are designed not only to conquer worry, fear and anxiety, but they will, at the same time, empower us with security and well-being.

In addition to giving us a feeling of empowerment, the encouragement found in God's Word will also help eliminate the maladies that seem to keep His children from the triumphal living He desires for them. God doesn't want any of His children living with low self-esteem, fear, despair and hopelessness. No one can claim victory as long as their life is entrenched in low self-esteem. There's no place in the Kingdom of God where despair and hopelessness are welcome. God established encouragement, just as He did faith, and He has called each of us to go forth and speak it into the lives of others, knowing full well that encouragement would play a necessary role in helping His children overcome the difficulties found in this world. It's important to note that Christ called Himself an *overcomer*, not a survivor; there's a distinct difference. Somehow John 16:33 would not hold the same meaning if it were written:

"In this world you will have trouble. But take heart I have *survived* the world."

It's not God's intent for His people to merely *cope* in this world; God's desire is for His people to live as victors in this world! That's what overcoming is. Some define victory as possessing fame or fortune; others see it more as rising above monumental obstacles or defeating great odds. And while those can be defined as victory according to man, it would be best to give you God's definition:

*For everyone born of God overcomes the world. This is the victory that has overcome the world, even our faith.*
*(1 John 5:4-5)*

John is stating that through our faith in God we have already experienced victory, the victory of overcoming the limitations and the restrictions of this world. This world states that death is eminent. God, however, demonstrated for us that while death to our bodies may be eminent, eternal life for our souls is reality. Talk about a victory!

God wants us to know the final outcome ahead of time for one reason. It's His desire for His children to exist in a state of victory every day. Many of us, though, aren't getting it. Instead of living in victory far too many exist in a state of oppression or depression. They're under the impression that victory is found in the job they have, the clothes they wear, the car they drive or the popularity they pursue. Little do they know that it's their pursuit of such things that actually keeps them from experiencing God's daily victory celebrations. People who live by this philosophy are held in bondage by their next purchase or their next promotion. Their idea of victory is wrapped up in something they can show their neighbor. That's not at all what God had in mind – unless what they intend to show their neighbor is the reality of their faith.

### Remember:
- Winning in this life is directly proportional to one thing: our obedience to the Word of God.
- There's no such thing as editing the Word of God.
- As children of light and possessors of God's Spirit, we are to assume the role of encourager and speak forth the inspiring words of Jesus.
- There's no place in the Kingdom of God where despair and hopelessness are welcome.

### Enacting your faith
It's imperative that we realize we don't need more faith. Any amount of faith given to us by our Father is sufficient for our lives. What we have to do is learn to enact it, put it into practice. The way we do that is three-fold. First, we have to recognize we have troubles (usually not too difficult to do). Then, we have to "cast" those troubles on God (a little more difficult). Finally, we have to let them (troubles) go by ignoring our tendency to be fearful of what the outcome might be (that's the hardest part). Being reminded of our faith in God, either through reading His Word or by having a friend come alongside and encourage us in God's Word, can make all the difference in the world.

# 28

# The Necessity of Encouraging

*After Paul and Silas came out of the prison, they*
*went to Lydia's house, where they met with the brothers*
*and encouraged them.*
*(Acts 16:40)*

Encouraging isn't just something we are called to do; it's something we need to do. We need to do it because, along with a list of other things, it keeps us from holding pity parties for ourselves. One of the greatest deterrents to our growth as a Christian is feeling sorry for our self. Self-pity deters us because it keeps us from realizing just how truly blessed we are. If we aren't able to recognize how blessed we are, there will be no thanksgiving in our lives. The Book of Psalms does a great job of teaching us to give thanks:

> *O Lord my God, I will give you thanks forever.*
> *(Psalm 30:12)*

In Hebrews we are told that without a thankful heart, it's impossible to worship God, the Creator of thanksgiving:

> *Let us be thankful, and so worship*
> *God acceptably with reverence and awe.*
> *(Hebrews 13:28)*

It's essential that we spend time being thankful for the blessings of life regardless of the circumstances we find ourselves in. That attitude does not come naturally. Our natural tendency is to see clearly the blessings of others but be so distracted by our own state of affairs, we fail to notice just how blessed we are. Only the maturity we receive in walking with Christ will give us the perspective we need to filter through our life and realize our ungrateful attitude has no basis. Without this godly perception, we'll tend to view blessings as nothing but answers to our selfish prayers. Then, when we don't receive the things we want, we begin to question why:

- "Why wasn't I promoted?"
- "Why do my bills pile up so fast?"
- "Why didn't anyone ask me?"
- "Why was I the only one singled out?"

When our focus is internal, it's easy to get into this mindset. When we're sitting around with little to do (the enemy loves an idle mind), we start thinking of all the times during our day when someone else got a break that we didn't, or we obsess over how unfair the hand is we've been dealt. This compulsion to fixate all our thinking on our own problems is stemmed in our flesh. Now, the flesh knows one thing and one thing only; it will pretty much do anything to get its own way. That's why Paul wrote what he did to the Roman Church. He knew he needed to be set free from himself if he was going to serve Jesus.

*What a wretched man I am! Who will rescue*
*me from this body of death?*
*(Romans 7:24)*

Paul was letting the Roman Christians – and Christians today – know how impossible it is to serve Christ and ourselves at the same time. Paul knew if he only listened to his flesh, he would never hear the call of God to come alongside his fellow man and bless him. We have to turn a deaf ear to our flesh when it starts whining about how God has forgotten all about us, and how He seems much more interested in blessing other people than He does us. Turning our flesh off when it starts into it's *all about me* package is essential to fulfilling our call to encourage others.

Learning to encourage others, regardless of where we find ourselves, takes incredible discipline. Nothing in all of Scripture has encouraged me more than the following testimony in Paul and Silas's journey for the Lord:

> *The crowd joined in the attack against Paul and Silas, and the*
> *magistrates ordered them to be stripped and beaten. After they had*
> *been severely flogged, they were thrown into prison, and the jailer*
> *was commanded to guard them carefully. Upon receiving such*
> *orders, he put them in the inner cell and fastened their feet in the*
> *stocks. About midnight Paul and Silas were praying and singing*
> *hymns to God, and the other prisoners were listening to them.*
> *(Acts 16:22-25)*

Those four verses contain incredibly more than a mere measure of encouragement. Here are two men who are obediently following the call of God and yet find themselves not blessed as one might expect, but persecuted. They are doing what they should be doing for the Lord, and their reward is what? A set of shackles and a good flogging? I can't help thinking what my attitude would be given their circumstances? Would I be singing God's praises after getting beaten and thrown into prison? You know, I don't think I want to answer that.

I'm looking for affirmation following one of my sermons, for crying out loud; I can only imagine what I'd be thinking if my congregation had me tossed in jail at the end of a service. (I really shouldn't be giving them any ideas.) We need to be asking ourselves the question: Do my circumstances determine my actions for the Lord? If they do, should they?

Are we to profess the goodness of God only when that profession earns us praise? That would certainly be a lot easier, but that's not what we're called to do. We're called to witness God's goodness regardless of the reaction we get from people. The apostle Paul wrote some pretty good guidelines for living out this philosophy.

> *Am I now trying to win the approval of men or of God? Or*
> *am I trying to please men? If I were still trying to please*
> *men, I would not be a servant of Christ.*
> *(Galatians 1:10)*

Paul and Silas didn't do what they did to please the people. Pleasing people will get you patted on the back, not flogged. Paul and Silas did what they did to please the Lord. I'm sure their flesh was crying out, "This is unfair! Where are you, God, when we really need you?" And while their flesh was screaming for attention, they were ignoring the obvious pain and their unmerited state of affairs. They chose instead to obediently follow the Spirit. They had a choice, and that choice was to praise God in the midst of their situation or curse God for their situation.

**God is to be blessed in all things**

How does this scriptural account, occurring two-thousand years ago, help us? It not only demonstrates that we can find ourselves unfairly treated while serving the Lord, but also it shows us that God can do amazing things as long as we keep our eyes on Him. The thing I've learned from Paul and Silas's experience is, if those guys can go through being stripped and beaten, shackled and flogged, and come out glorifying the Lord, I can find a way to get my eyes off myself and my nowhere-near- Paul-and-Silas's circumstances long enough to praise Him too.

I've come to discover, one of the utmost ways of offering praise to the Lord is by encouraging others in the midst of our trials. It's also one of the most impressionable ways to glorify the Lord. God must be seen as worthy of our praise no matter what the conditions are. Praising God after passing the bar exam or following the winning touchdown is good, but praising Him in the midst of our chemotherapy treatment will cause others to sit up and take notice. It's easy to thank Him and bless Him for the birth of our healthy child, but blessing Him as our child fights for his life in a neo-natal incubator is where the world shakes its collective head and wonders just who is this God. It's important to remember that God is to be blessed in all things, not just the things which make us feel good. The attitude of the world is to thank Him only after receiving everything they've asked for. The attitude of His children should be to thank Him regardless of what we receive.

**Praising God may lead others to God**

We read a portion of the Book of Acts earlier in this chapter. The remainder of Acts 16 further demonstrates the power we possess when our self-pity gets put on the shelf in lieu of God's praise. Upon reading the entire chapter, you see that the jailer who strapped Paul and Silas into their cell ended up receiving Christ as his Lord. Not only did he begin his eternal journey into God's Kingdom, but after inviting the "convicts" into his home, his entire family got saved as well.

One can make a strong case that the prayers and praise emanating from the disciples' cell served as the encouragement the jailer needed to make his decision to accept the Lord. He couldn't help but take notice of a God who enables His people to rejoice in the midst of pain and suffering. After all, these men should have been moaning and wailing, not giving thanks. He obviously wanted to know this same God on the level that Paul and Silas did, and acting on that desire he reached out to this God, and the rest was up to the Holy Spirit. He was so moved that his responsibility to Caesar took a backseat to his longing to know the Christ of Paul and Silas.

What great opportunities we have daily to encourage others through our praise! Are we taking advantage of these opportunities or squandering them? When faced with trials of our own, we can choose to moan and wail, or we can choose to glorify our Lord in Heaven. Moaning and wailing may get us temporary sympathy, but singing and praising God may lead others into eternal security.

These two encouragers weren't done. After being released from prison, Paul and Silas couldn't wait to go to the house of Lydia, where the other disciples were staying, and continue their quest of encouraging.

*After Paul and Silas came out of the prison, they went to Lydia's house, where they met with the brothers and encouraged them.*
*(Acts 16:40)*

That's another instance where I don't know if I could have done the same thing as Paul and Silas. I probably would have shown up at Lydia's house alright but not for the same reason. Instead of going there to tell them all about what God has done, I would have gone there to show them the wounds from my flogging. It would have been natural for me to peel off my shirt and show them the whip marks, or roll up my pant leg and point out the cuts on my ankles where the metal shackles dug into my flesh. I would have been working all kinds of angles in an attempt to get more than a little compassion. My motivation in going there would have been just a wee bit more self-centered than either Paul's or Silas' I'm afraid. Although I would have known better than to say it, my actions would have said it for me, "Hey, look what I'm doing for the Lord. I must be pretty spiritual, huh?" And while that is a more natural response to what happened to Paul and Silas, rarely will it yield any glory for the Lord.

**Many are experiencing the true hardships of life**

Earlier in Romans 12, we discussed how God gives His people certain spiritual gifts in an effort to edify His body of believers. One of those gifts we talked about was encouraging. The application of the verse, **"If it is encouraging, let him encourage"** (Romans 12:8) seems to say, "If you have the ability and the opportunity to encourage other people, then, by all means, do it!" This Scripture doesn't go on to list the various ways one can encourage. Paul did not expound upon how God's gift of encouragement is to be carried out. I believe that was purposeful.

It can be assumed, with good reason, Paul didn't want to limit God's encouragers. Paul did not say, "Encouragers are to share their encouragement by writing journals" or "Encouragers are to share their encouragement by testifying in church" or "Encouragers are to share their encouragement by organizing support groups." Had Paul done that, I'm afraid we would have assumed those examples to be the *only* ways to encourage rather than seeing them as *models* of encouragement. The truth is, we're limited in the ways we can encourage others only by the limitations of God; and since God is without limit, so too are the ways of exhorting and validating those around us. Each one of us is unique, and every day we are placed in unique circumstances. God has left it to His divinely unique children to come up with our own original ways of encouraging each other. We can invest those unique opportunities for the Lord or squander them on ourselves; the choice is truly ours.

It was never my intention in writing this book to tell others *how* they should encourage one another, but rather to illustrate the importance any and all encouragement can play in the lives of people, all people, especially those experiencing the true hardships of life. And trust me; there is no shortage of people experiencing hardships.

### God's mercy is sufficient

My Aunt Ish is one of those people who has had probably more than her share of the true hardships of life. She's a tremendous source of encouragement for me. She really is my aunt, but her name isn't really Ish. It's Odessa. She picked up the name Ish in high school because her haircut resembled that of the leader of Kay Kaiser's band, Ish Kabibble. If you aren't old enough to have voted for Eisenhower, then you'll just have to take my word for it. Aunt Ish is a living, breathing example of encouragement for everyone who knows her story.

My effort in using my aunt's life as an encouraging example for others is not to garner support and sympathy for her (that would be the last thing she'd want), but rather to show others, who have gone through similar suffering, how their lives can be an inspiration to those around them. Some eighty-four-year-olds look and act like they're eighty-four, and some look and act a whole lot less. Aunt Ish is on the side of the whole lot less. Active in her church and quite social in her activities, it's not easy to find her at home. The only way you can be sure she is at home is to check Ohio State's football schedule. If their game is being televised, then she'll be home. Now, in my estimation, Aunt Ish could have been an anchor on ESPN had it been around in the '60s. I've coached football for thirty-seven years and there are times I'm hard pressed to answer some of her questions about the game.

Her enchantment regarding sports goes way back, but it's not the reason she encourages me so much. The reason she encourages me has to do with not only what, but how, she has endured the last twenty years of her life. It was that many years ago that my aunt's oldest son Gary contracted HIV. It was relatively early in the outbreak of the disease and many of the medicines they have now were not available. My cousin's HIV quickly developed into full blown AIDS, and he wasn't spared from the debilitation, or the pain, this disease can cause. My aunt and uncle stayed by my cousin's side through it all, as any loving parent would. They grieved together and encouraged one another through some extremely excruciating times. After what seemed like an eternity, my cousin Gary, following months and even years of battling this disease, succumbed to death. People who've experienced the death of an offspring say that burying a child is one of the most difficult times a parent can ever experience.

Not long after that, my Uncle Bob, Aunt Ish's husband, began experiencing congestive heart failure. He went through two defibulators and a number of surgeries, but ultimately his heart gave out. That left the family with just my aunt and her youngest son Rob, who lived four hundred miles away in Chicago. One day Aunt Ish discovered a lump during self-examination, and after a biopsy was performed, it was revealed she had breast cancer. At almost the same time, her son Rob went to his doctor to have some skin irregularities checked. The doctors discovered immediately that he had an aggressive form of melanoma. My aunt spent the next few years of her life between home and Chicago in an effort to be with her son as much as possible.

When we were able to finally convince Rob to come home, he took a turn for the worse, and before we knew it, my aunt was planning the funeral of her second child. I'm not trying to portray her as though she is the poster child for adversity and suffering. There are, I'm sure, many others who have seen more hardship. It's just that I know the reality of her pain. I've witnessed it and I've shared in it. And through it all, she has relied upon her faith, the real source of my encouragement. To know that God's mercy is sufficient in seeing His children though anything, even something as painful as what she's endured, encourages me and strengthens my faith. And to know that same mercy is also available to me brings a peace that's impossible to describe. You see, I know first-hand that God is the source of my aunt's strong faith, and if she isn't disappointed in the Lord, I will never be either.

**Everyone wants to know they're contributing**

Maybe this account of my aunt's life has caused you to see some of the difficulties you have had to endure in a little different light. Maybe you have never seen yourself as an encouraging person before. Maybe your circumstances have required so much of your attention that the thought never occurred to you how others could possibly be encouraged just by watching you live out your life. Don't be so quick to dismiss that possibility. Chances are there have been a good many people who have watched you and taken note of your attitude in facing your difficulties. It's more than likely your positive attitude in facing them has served to encourage a number of others.

When I shared with my aunt how her life has been an inspiration to me and to my family, she seemed astonished. It was something she had never even considered. That goes to show you that you never know the potential impact your life has on other people.

Just because you may not be out there encouraging others through testimonies and sermons doesn't mean you cannot be an encourager. If there is someone you know who inspires you by how they live their life, someone whose attitude is a source of encouragement, please tell them. It may give them the inspiration they're looking for to make it through another day. By letting them know how much you have benefited from their attitude toward life could help them come to understand there may be a reason they are going through whatever it is they're going through. Knowing their hardships served to help others and that they were not in vain will give others purpose.

There are many people who see absolutely no good coming from their life, people who shake their fists at God and question, "Why? Why is my life so painful?" By sharing with them how encouraging their life has been to you might be exactly what they need to hear. Everyone wants to know what contribution, if any, their life is making. The last thing you ever want to do is keep quiet about what someone's attitude or living testimony is doing or has done for you. Tell them. Speak it out. In doing so, you are fulfilling two needs: your need to encourage and their need to be encouraged.

*Remember...*
- Encouraging isn't just something we are called to do; it is something we need to do.

- We're only limited in the ways we can encourage others by the limitations of God.
- It's impossible to serve Christ and ourselves at the same time.

### *If you don't tell them, who will?*

Most of us never think of ourselves as models of encouragement. Many of us just live our lives and battle our difficulties hoping to experience the least amount of pain as possible. When you think about it that way, life almost becomes something to avoid rather than something to cherish. God has given us life abundantly, not life inadequately. Too often our perception of an inadequate life is realized because of our failure to see how the problems and pains we endure can ever be seen as anything positive. That's why encouraging is a necessity. People need to know there is purpose in the struggles and strains of life. Tell someone you know, someone who has been an inspiration to you for how they live their life. Tell them how encouraged you are watching them go through life, cherishing it rather than avoiding it. Don't wait either; do it today. As a matter of fact, why not do it right now?

## 29

# Encouraging ala Mickey Goldmill

*Therefore encourage one another and build each other up.*
*(1Thessalonians 5:11)*

When it comes to having seen the movie *Rocky,* there are generally two camps of viewers: those who stood cheering in the movie theaters back in the '70s, and those who have stood cheering from their living rooms watching the VCR or the DVD version. There is no third camp, since virtually every American has seen the movie at least once. I think there's a law on the books in more than one state that says you can be deported for never having watched *Rocky.*

It remains an amazingly inspiring film despite its incredible low budget and its premise that a five-foot-six, punch-drunk-has-been can seriously challenge for the heavyweight championship of the world. Its popularity of course is rooted in the theme of the underdog rising up and achieving despite insurmountable and overwhelming odds. By the way, I'm holding out for *Rocky VII* where Rocky Balboa decides to move to Cleveland, become an NFL quarterback and lead the Browns to the Super Bowl. But then, who's going to believe that?

And though most viewers tend to credit Rocky himself and his eccentric workouts of beating up on hapless sides of beef, chasing chickens and running around with a telephone pole on his shoulder for preparing him to take on the World Champion, a more extensive look reveals that Rocky's preparation and progress would never have taken place without the inspiration of having someone in his life believe in him. As much physical preparation as Rocky put in to his fight, I hold out that without someone in

208

his camp motivating and encouraging the "Italian Stallion" and reminding him that he indeed belongs in that ring, there's no telling how long his match would have lasted. You see, we can be the most confident and physically capable person alive, but if we're always out there battling alone, there's going to come a time when our confidence and our ability come up a bit short. Those are the times we need a Mickey Goldmill in our lives.

The late Burgess Meredith played Rocky's elderly trainer, Mickey Goldmill, in the original movie, as well as the following two sequels, and it's his character I credit for much of Rocky's on-screen success. Obviously Rocky had ability and Rocky had heart, but as every one of us discovers sooner or later, it's going to take more than that when we find ourselves up against the "Apollo Creeds" of the world. Throughout the movie we find Rocky continually questioning his own ability. There are even times when he thinks it's a possibility that by stepping into the ring against the World Champion he could get himself killed.

What enables Rocky to go on despite his wavering confidence is the encouragement his grizzled trainer instills in him. Now, no one would ever accuse Mickey of being Mister Sensitive; there are occasions when he verbally abuses Rocky, however, his intentions of bringing out the very best in his fighter are never in question. Mickey had always believed in Rocky; he just felt that Rocky squandered his talents and his opportunity to be the very best he could be by making so many poor choices in his life. Now given this once-in-a-lifetime opportunity for the fighter to redeem himself, Mickey becomes Rocky's alter ego in an attempt to enable Rocky to live out his dream.

### Attitude is invaluable when going into battle

That's the message I want you to see, the message of how one person, speaking inspiring and affirming words into the life of another person can motivate that person to not only stand up and face his opponents, but to eventually rise up and defeat them. I know it's "just a movie," but if we were to get honest here, everyone of us have run into a Rocky Balboa or two in our lives, people we know who possess a certain amount of ability and heart but who find themselves questioning that heart when faced with what could be seen as insoluble odds. One thing that can contribute in spurring them on to rise above those odds is to hear that someone else believes in them.

It was apparent early in the movie that Rocky never knew Mickey believed he had what it takes to be a champion. Rocky never knew it because Mickey never told him. Once Rocky learned that this veteran trainer recognized and respected his talent, his attitude in believing he belonged in that ring changed dramatically. Attitude is such an invaluable trait when going into battle. For example:

- Healthcare professionals tell us how the mind-set of their patients, when going through therapy and treatment, can have an amazing influence on the success or failure of their recovery.
- Military leaders make it a practice to address their men with uplifting and inspiring words preceding their march into battle, knowing the importance confidence plays in combat.
- Athletic coaches carefully plan out their pre-game pep talks in an effort to say just the right thing that will give their players the emotional edge as the game draws near.

We all realize the importance of our mind-set when attempting to achieve success in every realm of life, yet how often do we send our spouses, our children or our friends out to face adversity with those much-needed words of inspiration and encouragement?

"Honey I believe in you. I've seen you at your best and let me tell you, there's nothing you can't accomplish once you put your mind to it."

God calls us to fulfill the role of a Mickey Goldmill for those around us because He knows there will come a time when each one of us will be in that ring facing the trials brought on by the likes of "Clubber Langs" (*Rocky III*) and "Ivan Dragos" (*Rocky IV*).

Scripture doesn't pull any punches when it comes to preparing us for the times ahead.

> *Dear friends, do not be surprised at the painful trial*
> *you are suffering as though something strange*
> *were happening to you.*
> *(1 Peter 4:12)*

Many of those times will be dark, times when we might even question our own faith because of the circumstances and situations that have befallen us. Having a Mickey Goldmill or two in our lives during these times will be an invaluable source of motivation. By reminding us that the truth found in God's Word applies personally to us and our situation, they can assist us in not only enduring the pain of the moment, but they can help us in eventually overcoming it as well.

You can probably think of at least one person right now who is going through something where they could use an inspiring trainer in their corner. Is there any reason *you* can't be their Mickey Goldmill? I'm sure you could come up with a dozen reasons why you can't, but if you were to be honest, how many of those reasons are valid? And even if you can't think of something to say on your own, you have the Bible, an entire book filled with the promises and encouragement of an all-loving, all-compassionate God.

There will be those who think it's more than a stretch to use the character of Mickey Goldmill to demonstrate how coming alongside someone else and speaking into them words of inspiration and motivation will enable them to achieve despite great odds. And I agree, the dialogue of the movie is from the fantasy world of Hollywood, but I would also argue the movie's message is anything but fantasy. I've coached competitive sports long enough to know that more often than you may think, players and teams can and do achieve despite great odds stacked against them.

I have also discovered the common element found in the vast majority of these "David defeating Goliath" outcomes. The common element is people, people not unlike you and me, people who are willing and able to impart a message of confidence and inspiration into the lives of those who desperately need it. All you have to do is read the morning sports page to realize that people and teams who have been given virtually no chance of succeeding in a game of competition do find occasions when they get to take their place in the winner's circle. And if you trace their path to that winner's circle, my bet is that you'll discover more than one person who has influenced that athlete or that team to go on despite what it looked like on paper.

The term "to go on" is the key. Without "going on," nothing can be achieved. No one has ever succeeded by giving up; no one has ever achieved by throwing in the towel; no one has ever overcome by refusing to go forth. The universal component shared by every person who has ever prevailed against a powerful and relentless enemy is that they "went on." How will you know if you can achieve unless you "go on"? There's no question that "to go on" becomes a whole lot easier when there's someone standing over you inspiring you to get up off the canvass and back into the fight.

**Winning every battle is not reality**

One of the things I love about the original *Rocky* movie is that if you remember, Rocky Balboa lost the fight. I wanted him to win just like everyone who watched that movie wanted him to win. And as much as we all hoped he'd knock more than just the arrogance out of Apollo Creed, Rocky's defeat became the most realistic part of the movie. Winning every battle we face is not reality. God doesn't promise us that we will win every battle; He just promises us that we (those who have chosen to trust in Him) win the war!

Our enemy remains relentless in waging battle after battle in an attempt to demoralize and discourage those fighting "the good fight." His hope is that we will give up trying out of sheer exhaustion. What can keep us from waving our white flag are the inspiring words spoken to us by our friends. Encouraging one another to *keep on keeping on* despite the unrelenting attacks of the enemy can easily be likened to the trainer's role in a prize fight. After each round, the fighter wearily comes back to his corner, maybe with a cut over one eye and a bruise under the other to hear what his trainer has to say. "You're doin' great! Just keep bobbin' and weavin', and when he goes to throw that big right hand, counter it with a couple of jabs and a good shot to the body. It looks like he's starting to tire out. I believe in you; I know it isn't easy, but listen, keep your eye on the prize and you're destined to come out on top."

That's our role as encouragers. The trainer obviously isn't coaching the fighter to lose or even to survive; he's coaching him to win, to claim the prize, to keep his eye on the reason he climbed into the ring in the first place. Encouragers are needed to remind us that our goal should never be to merely cope, but to follow Christ into becoming an overcomer in this world. There aren't many successful prize fighters who take with them into the ring the goal to just make it through the fight. If they don't begin at the onset of their training routine with their eyes fixed on winning, confident that their training methods will adequately prepare them for their battle, then the chances of them raising their arms in triumph at the end of that battle are slim at best. God calls us to victory, and that means before we can attain that victory we must first set a goal of success. That goal of success must also be based entirely upon God and His Word.

*Be strong and very courageous. Be careful to obey all the law…*
*that you may be successful wherever you go. Do not let this Book*
*of the Law depart from your mouth; meditate on it day and night*

> *so that you may do everything written in it. Then you will*
> *be prosperous and successful.*
> *(Joshua 1:7-8)*

Now, along the way we may have to adapt and evolve our plans some-what because of temporary setbacks; however, the ultimate goal of coming out victorious for the Lord never changes. The best part is that the outcome of success in our life isn't left to the opinion of three humans sitting at ringside adding up the number of punches thrown. Our judgment comes from One who has gone through it all before us, and He bases our outcome not on the outward physical success we may or may not realize, but upon the inward motivation of our hearts.

> *The Lord does not look at the things man looks at.*
> *Man looks at the outward appearance, but the*
> *Lord looks at the heart.*
> *(1 Samuel 16:7)*

There was never a question that Rocky had heart. It was the attitude of his heart that formed the premise of the movie. It was also evident that the courage that comprised so much of Rocky's heart was due in part to the inspiration of Mickey Goldmill. If you didn't come away from that movie totally inspired, then I'll be praying for you to awaken from your coma sometime soon. Ultimately it didn't even matter that Rocky lost the fight, because in the minds of the millions of viewers, he won the war!

Take another look at that Scripture from First Samuel. It takes enormous pressure off of us, doesn't it? Imagine going through life no longer worrying about winning every battle you have to face because in your heart-of-hearts you know you have already won the war! That mindset can be our reality as long as we keep in perspective God and His Word. What will also help immensely is having like-minded brothers and sisters coming alongside us through this battle of life, encouraging and affirming us, especially when we so often stumble back to our corner of the ring bruised and weary.

Listen, it's probably a good bet that your opponent isn't someone you can stand toe to toe with trading punches. Your opponent, more than likely, isn't one person or even people at all. It doesn't matter. Regardless of your opponent or the odds stacked against you, regardless of what it may look like on the surface, regardless of how much or how little time we're told we have left, we have an all-loving merciful Father in heaven who reassures us that the canvass ring we call Earth is not where life ends.

*Then I saw a new heaven and a new earth...And I heard a loud voice*
*from the throne saying, "Now the dwelling of God is with men, and*
*He will live with them. He will wipe every tear from their eyes. There*
*will be no more death or mourning or crying or pain, for the old*
*order of things has passed away."*
*(Revelation 21:1,3-4)*

Just like in *Rocky*, there is a sequel to this life as well. Unlike the movie versions, only one sequel is needed. Mercifully and graciously the script has already been written, the outcome already determined. Those who trust in the Lord today never have to question their own ability or weigh whether or not the odds align in their favor. Eternal life is not about rolling the dice, crossing our fingers or making a wish. Eternal life is about listening to and believing in the One True Creator and Sustainer of all life. Holding on to the hope of our salvation is all the training and preparation we're ever going to need. And holding on to that hope is made a whole lot easier when we have people in our lives willing to put an encouraging arm around us and speak into us words that inspire us to go on when we're convinced we can't.

*Remember...*
- Encouragers are needed to remind us that our goal should never be to merely cope, but to follow Christ into becoming an overcomer in this world.
- People will never know how much we believe in them unless we tell them.
- No one has ever succeeded by giving up; no one has ever achieved by throwing in the towel; no one has ever overcome by refusing to go on.

*Here's your chance*
Whether or not you remember the Mickey Goldmill character from *Rocky* doesn't really matter. As a matter of fact, it doesn't really matter if you've never seen the movie. The only thing that does matter is possessing a love for people and a desire to see each one of them live life to the fullest. That's God's desire for every one of us.

*I have come that they may have life, and have it to the full.*
*(John 10:10)*

One sure way of having life to the full is by imparting a sense of con-fidence and encouragement into the lives of those desperately in need of a Mickey Goldmill or two!

# Encouragement to Go

Has *Unleashing the Power of Encouragement* caused you to look at your life, or maybe your purpose in life, a little differently than before? Yes? Great! That was my prayer. (It's so exciting when prayers are answered.)

Okay, so what are you going to do about it? With knowledge comes responsibility. There's no way you can continue passing up opportunity after opportunity to inspire, affirm, restore or encourage now that you possess the awareness of what that inspiration, affirmation, and restoration can do for others.

Don't ever believe that someone in need of encouragement crosses your path by coincidence. It's a strong possibility that it's God who has you crossing paths. He may have placed you there so that you can hold out His words of nourishment and life to someone desperately in need of them.

My brand new grandson has caused me to see life moving by more quickly than I ever have before. Holding him in my arms, I am made glaringly aware there are only so many opportunities we are afforded in our time here. I don't want to allow even one of those opportunities to slip away. Will you stand with me, seizing every moment as though it is our last, and allow an unleashing of this inner power to transform the hearts and lives of all of God's children?

# 101 Examples of Encouragement

The following examples of encouragement merely scratch the surface. My guess is it will be no time at all before you compile your own 101 ways to encourage others. I can tell you this, blessings will come to you in the endeavor.

1. "I can always count on you."
2. "Your friendship means a lot to me."
3. "I value your opinion."
4. "What a blessing you are."
5. "You're always thinking of other people."
6. "I can't believe how much you've matured."
7. "Can I do something to help you?"
8. "No matter what, I've got your back."
9. "I know of very few people who would have done what you did."
10. "You're such a good person."
11. "You always look so nice."
12. "You have certainly earned my trust."
13. "I enjoy spending time with you."
14. "Boy, are you good with your hands."
15. "You always have such good suggestions."
16. "You seem to go out of your way for other people."
17. "I wish I could be more like you."
18. "What makes you such a likable person?"
19. "You have such good taste."
20. "You have a way of making people feel welcome."
21. "You're always so even-tempered."
22. "I trust your judgment."
23. "Where do you get that kind of strength?"

24. "Can you help me be more like that?"
25. "Have you always been so optimistic?"
26. "You could find something positive in anyone."
27. "You're able to communicate so well."
28. "Is there anything you *can't* do?"
29. "I always feel better after talking with you."
30. "You're more attractive to me today than the day we got married."
31. "I see your potential as unlimited."
32. "I've always been able to count on good advice from you."
33. "No one understands me the way you do."
34. "Your compassion for people is exemplary"
35. "You are the real deal."
36. "You're the best looking pastor I've ever seen." (This is my personal favorite.)
37. "I'm a better person for having you as a friend."
38. "Words cannot express how great you make me feel."
39. "God has to be proud of the person you've become."
40. "People seem to radiate to you."
41. "How do you keep yourself looking so young?"
42. "You always did have a knack for making me laugh."
43. "You've done a great job raising your kids."
44. "You are someone I can confide in."
45. "You're awesome!"
46. "Wow, you're talented!"
47. "Where can I buy your book?" (My second favorite.)
48. "You did that all by yourself?"
49. "I'm proud to call you my friend."
50. "My mom says you're a good influence on me."
51. "Excellent!"
52. "I trust you."
53. "I appreciate your effort."
54. "I'm standing in the presence of greatness."
55. "If I can do it, so can you."
56. "I need you in my life."
57. "You are one thoughtful person."
58. "What did I ever do without you?"
59. "How do you stay so positive?"
60. "What amazing potential you have."
61. "I see the Lord at work in you."
62. "Wow, do you clean up well!"

63. "I could learn a lot from you."
64. "I'm in awe of your patience."
65. "Your heart always seems to be in the right place."
66. "You always have time for people."
67. "I've never heard you say anything bad about anyone."
68. "There's something about you that seems to attract people."
69. "I appreciate the way you listen to my problems."
70. "I hope you know how special you truly are."
71. "What do you think?"
72. "I don't believe you have a negative bone in your body"
73. "Life just seems better when I'm with you."
74. "Can you teach me to do that?"
75. "You're the first person I called."
76. "Outstanding!"
77. "Is there any way I could clone you?"
78. "I don't know how you manage."
79. "You inspire me."
80. "You make me want to be a better person."
81. "Reid, I didn't know you had three daughters." (Michele's favorite.)
82. "That was better than good; that was great!"
83. "Compared to you, I've got a long way to go."
84. "It's the little things you do for me."
85. "You've got to be in the running for Parent-of-the-Year."
86. "God made you with an extra measure of patience."
87. "How do you do all that you do?"
88. "You're as honest as they come."
89. "Your children are so well-mannered."
90. "I get so much out of your teaching."
91. "What great balance you have in your life."
92. "Your son is so gifted." (My mother's favorite.)
93. "Your energy is contagious."
94. "You never seem to have a bad day."
95. "I just love your passion for life."
96. "I'm here for you."
97. "We'll get through this together."
98. "Your generosity overwhelms me."
99. "You just always seem so hopeful."
100. "Your work is exceptional."
101. "_____" (Here's where you start your own list.)

# Epilogue

*May our Lord Jesus Christ himself and God our*
*Father, who loved us and by his grace gave us eternal*
*encouragement and good hope, encourage your hearts*
*and strengthen you in every good deed and word.*
*(2 Thessalonians 2:16-17)*

The writing of this book has caused me to become not only more aware of how important encouraging others can be, but also it has enlightened me as to the vast number of opportunities afforded us every day to do so. My hope in sharing this with all of you is to affect a personal stirring, one that awakens your desire to see people around you become validated and their lives enhanced, a stirring that awakens you to the privilege of watching people walk away with a renewed sense of who they were created to be after sharing a moment with you.

The truth is, we all carry with us an amazing amount of potential everywhere we go. This potential has the ability to spiritually and emotionally nourish those around us. However, this valuable potential if it is stored and never released is nothing more than a hoarding away of one of God's most precious gifts to us, the gift of encouragement. Whatever your reason has been for not sharing it before now is no longer important. The only thing that matters from this moment on is your commitment to release your encouragement at every opportunity.

It's God's desire to use you, and one of the most fulfilling ways He will do so is by using your voice to speak life into another human being. The thought of God accomplishing His will via your life should not only invigorate you, it should enable you to see the incredible purpose in your own creation as well. Imagine, the Eternal King of the Universe using you to assist Him in bringing forth His perfect plan. Keep in mind, while God and His plan to use people in speaking forth encouragement into the hearts and lives of others is perfect, those chosen to do so are anything but. This inevitably means that along the way we are going to take this perfect plan of God and combine it with our imperfections. But that can be the best part. You see, by relying on the power and strength of God and not on our own limited abilities to carry it out, we will see a one-hundred percent success rate!

*Every good and perfect gift is from above.*
*(James 1:17)*

# About the Author

R eid Lamport has been a special education teacher in the public schools for the past thirty-seven years. During this tenure, he has coached four varsity sports, won a national championship, and has been inducted into both the Poland Seminary High School and the Ohio High School Coaches Hall-of-Fame.

For almost four decades, Reid has enthusiastically fulfilled his role as teacher and coach by encouraging and motivating thousands of students and athletes to rise above their earthly talents and circumstances, and become the best they can be.

This passion for affirming those around him carries over to his role as pastor. He is the founder of The Church of the Rock in Poland, Ohio where he has served as Senior Pastor for the last eleven years.

Along with his many daily responsibilities, his talent for inspiring audiences remains in high demand. In his book, *Unleashing the Power of Encouragement*, Reid shares the principles, as well as the responsibilities, of becoming encouragers to those around us.

Reid's wife, Michele, serves as the music executive of their church and is an administrative assistant and huddle coordinator with the Steel Valley Fellowship of Christian Athletes in Youngstown. Reid and Michele have three adult children: Reid, 25; Jessica, 26; and Katie, 29, who along with her husband, Nick, gave birth on October 7, 2010 to Evan Reid Glatzer, the most handsome grandbaby ever!

To contact the author to share your personal stories of encouragement or to request information about having Reid speak to your group or organization write to him at: rlamport@unleashingthepowerofencouragement. com or call 330-518-0006.

9 781613 791943